jetlag travel guide

Molvanîa

A LAND UNTOUCHED BY MODERN DENTISTRY...

ATLANTIC BOOKS
LONDON

First published in 2003 in Australia
by Hardie Grant Books in conjunction with Working Dog Pty Ltd

First published in Great Britain in 2004
by Atlantic Books, an imprint of Grove Atlantic Ltd.

Text © Working Dog Pty Ltd 2003

Photographs © 2003 (see p 4)

Maps & Illustrations © Working Dog Pty Ltd 2003

JETLAG ™   ™   Molvania ™

1 3 5 7 9 8 6 4 2

A CIP catalogue record for this book is available from the British Library.

1 84354 232 3

Printed in Great Britain by CPI Bath

Atlantic Books
An imprint of Grove Atlantic Ltd
Ormond House
26-27 Boswell Street
London
WC1N 3JZ

Szlengro!

[Welcome!]

Written by Santo Cilauro, Tom Gleisner & Rob Sitch
Edited by Martine Lleonart
Cover and text design Trisha Garner
Maps by Trisha Garner
Illustrations by Kim Roberts pp 13, 16, 67, 76
Printed and bound by CPI Bath

PHOTOGRAPHY:
Giuseppe Albo (deceased) pp 18, 25, 51, 60, 107, 140, 141, 146,167; **Bill Bachman** pp 3, 8, 17, 28, 37, 38, 39, 42, 46, 52, 54, 61, 74, 77, 81, 86, 87, 108, 109, 123, 131, 143; **Margherita Cilauro** pp 12, 23, 33, 48, 57, 73, 81, 89, 96, 97, 106, 115, 144, 154; **Santo Cilauro** pp 10-11, 15, 18, 22, 24, 26, 29, 30, 32, 34, 36, 44-45, 56, 62-63, 67, 70, 73, 77, 82, 83, 85, 88-89, 90, 95, 100, 116, 117, 118-19, 122, 129, 132, 138, 139, 156, 157, 161, 165, 171; **Emmanuel Santos** pp 22, 33, 92, 111, 117, 121, 128, 138; **Tom Gleisner** pp 21, 23, 38, 44, 58, 61, 64, 66, 72, 78, 99, 130, 133, 151, 155, 158, 165; **Pauline Hirsh** pp 113, 144-145, 171, inside back cover ('Surviving Moustaschistan', 'Sailing the Syphollos Straits'); **Lonely Planet Images** pp 9, 28, 55, 142, 148; **Working Dog** pp 7, 14, 31, 40, 41,107, 149, 174-75, 176, inside back cover ('Viva San Sombrero!', 'Aloha Takki Tikki', 'Let's go Bongoswana', 'Getting Round the Tofu Islands').

THE AUTHORS WOULD LIKE TO THANK:
The family of G. Albo, Liam Bradley, La Canna family, Mr & Mrs A. Caruso & family, Debra Choate, Ciccarone family, Cilauro family (especially Vito and Nonno Santo), Kate Cody, Rees Cornwall, Frances Forrest, Sandy Grant, David Herman, Michael Hirsh, Pauline Hirsh, Jane Kennedy, Simon Kuszninczuk, Luisa Laino, the town of Licodia Eubea, Lost Dogs Home, Simone Martin, Susannah Mott, Billy Pinnell, Marianne Raftopoulos, Amanda Seiffert, Greg Sitch, Julie Thomas, Polly Watkins.

Contents

THE AUTHORS

Rick

Rick van Dugan Born in Missouri, Rick always dreamed of travelling the world and, at the age of 18, begged his folks to let him spend a year overseas. So enthusiastic about the concept were his parents that they agreed to send him for three. Since that time Rick has been wandering the planet earning his living as a travel writer and freelance photographer. He has worked on numerous guidebooks, including *Baltic Europe*, *Czech Mate!* and *Kazakhstan on a Dollar a Month*.

Philippe

Philippe Miseree A professional traveller since his youth, there is not a city or town Philippe has not recently been disappointed by. No matter how obscure the destination you can bet he has been there before you and found it not half as good as it was in the 1970s. His earlier works include *Turkey Before it was Spoilt*, *India the Hard Way*, *South-East Asia on Less Than You Need* and *Unnecessarily Tough Travel*. Philippe helped compile our 'Complaints' section.

Olga

Olga Stryzki Born in California, Olga got the taste for travel early when as a young child her parents took her to Europe and left her there. She then found her way to Israel where she worked on a kibbutz for several weeks before being exchanged as a hostage with the PLO. A graduate in Political Science at UCLA, Olga lists her interests as Women's Studies, Women in History and Ice Hockey. She contributed to the sections on Molvanian women and spent the rest of her time complaining about the lack of disabled facilities.

Trudi

Trudi Dennes Trudi has lived and worked in Japan for over 10 years. She now works in the department of classical history at Tokyo University. Trudi has never visited Molvania and was assigned to this guide due to a staffing error.

Recz

Recz Jzervec A native Molvanian, Recz was born in the country's north and grew up there, only leaving at the age of 12 in order to avoid active military service.

Andy 'The Animal'

Andy 'The Animal' Wilson A native of Brisbane, Australia, Andy's first taste of overseas travel was an end-of-year trip to Bali with his amateur football team. What was supposed to be a two-week holiday turned into a year away, most of that time being spent in a Denpasar prison on charges of setting fire to a monk. By the time he was released the travel-bug had bit and Andy set out across South-East Asia on an alcohol-fuelled odyssey. After returning to Australia he decided to write a book about his experiences overseas but discovered he couldn't remember any. Since then Andy has had his visa cancelled in over 30 countries and can speak seven languages fluently when drunk. At last report he was in Afghanistan fighting with the Taliban. Andy helped compile the sections on nightlife and Molvanian beer-halls.

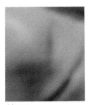

Horst
(photo courtesy Horst)

Many of the photographs in this book were taken by **Horst von Fluegel**, a keen traveller who only took up photography a few years ago. Despite the lack of any formal training, Horst has approached his work with enormous focus, a quality somewhat lacking in much of his pictorial output.

We Were Wrong! There is a spelling error on p151. The reference to 'rustic features' should in fact read 'rusty features'.

INTRODUCTION

Despite being one of the smallest countries in Europe, the **Republic of Molvania** has much to offer the discerning tourist. Panoramic scenery, magnificent neoclassical architecture and centuries of devotion to fine culture are, admittedly, all in short supply. But the intrepid traveller will still find plenty to enjoy within this unique, landlocked nation state – from the capital **Lutenblag**, with its delightful gas-powered tram network, to the heavily-forested **Postenwalj Mountains** in the south, where visitors can share a glass of locally brewed *zeerstum* (garlic brandy) while watching a traditionally-dressed peasant labourer beat his mule.

Molvania, the world's number one producer of beetroot and the birthplace of whooping cough, is a country steeped in history and everywhere here the past is beautifully preserved, such as in towns like **Gyrorik** where you'll find one of the oldest nuclear reactors still operating in the world. As far as buildings and public monuments go Molvania is doubly blessed, having experienced two architectural golden ages: a **Gothic period** under Holy Roman Emperor Charles IV and the late 1950s during which its Soviet-inspired love affair with non-reinforced concrete left an indelible mark on the urban landscape.

For the environmentally-minded, Molvania has enthusiastically embraced the concept of **eco-tourism** and, at the time of writing, numerous 'green lodges' were under construction, many deep within the fragile temperate forests of the country's north-east from whose timber they are also constructed.

The Royal Molvanian Folk Ensemble perform their traditional 'Biljardjig' ('Dance of the Billiard Cues').

A Molvanian peasant laboriously applies expiry dates to an egg at a local supermarket.

Of course, Molvania is also a country very much in touch with its modern side and cities like Lutenblag boast one of the **hippest nightclub scenes** in Europe. Here you'll see trendy, young Molvanian students dancing the night away to the sounds of a *fzdari* band (described by one visitor as 'techno-trance meets the *mazurka*') or perhaps take a tour of the massive automotive plant in **Bardjov**, where proud workers produce Molvania's national car, the *Skumpta*, with its distinctively stylish plywood interior trim.

Food lovers will be well catered for on any trip to this part of the world and Molvanian cuisine has certainly come a long way from the time when you could only find a few greasy, dimly-lit and **over-priced cafes** in the centre of Lutenblag. Nowadays such establishments have sprung up everywhere throughout the country.

Whatever you're looking for, chances are you'll find it in Molvania. All you need is this guide plus a few vaccinations* and you're ready to go!

* *For cholera, typhoid, diphtheria, hepatitis A, hepatitis B, polio, tuberculosis, hepatitis C, meningitis, malaria, tetanus, dengue fever and tickborne encephalitis. Those planning to travel into the countryside might also consider an anthrax shot.*

HISTORY

Although Slavic tribes probably occupied what is now Molvania in the 5th century, the first recorded reference to the country came in AD721 when the Prince of Molvanskia, **Nikod I**, declared himself lord of an empire taking in not only his own country, but Prussia, Germany and much of Scandinavia. It was an ambitious claim from a ruler who had just turned 12 years old and his expansionist reign lasted barely a few weeks.

The Middle Ages saw Molvania invaded by numerous armies, including the Goths, Tatars, Turks, Huns, Balts, Lombards and even a surprisingly militant band of Spanish nuns, before Molvania's first king and patron saint **Fyodor I**, set about unifying his country by killing off as many of its citizens as he could. Those not murdered or imprisoned were forced into teaching.

The empire converted to Christianity with the arrival of the missionary **St Parthag** in AD863 but reverted to paganism as soon as he left the following year. During the Dark Ages Molvania enjoyed a short period as a Muslim country, but the Koran's strict teachings against drinking, violence and **extra-marital sex** never caught on with the local population.

A baptismal font featuring one of Molvania's earliest martyrs, St Stripa (born AD 829 – excommunicated AD 863).

Molvania experienced a brief flowering of Renaissance culture, with some historians putting the actual period down to about three weeks towards the end of 1503. But there is certainly evidence of a renewed interest in art and culture beyond this time and during the 1520s one of Europe's most enlightened universities was built in the country's north at **Motensparg**, which offered courses in ancient Greek and Latin as well as wrestling scholarships.

In 1541 a peasant army attempted to turn on the landowners but the uprising was suppressed and the leader Gyidor Dvokic burned alive on a red-hot iron spike, giving rise to the modern Molvanian witticism '*eich zdern clakka yastenhach!*' (literally 'my rectum feels as if a great heat is being applied'). During this time the country consisted of numerous **semi-independent principalities** and city-states preoccupied with internal quarrels. In 1570 an attempt was made to bring these separate regions together but no-one could agree on a place to hold the meeting and the country was eventually plunged into the **Twenty Years War**, a conflict that actually ran for only six months.

The 17th century saw Molvania divided into various **fiefdoms**, each under the control of a despotic ruler who would ruthlessly crush the slightest sign of unrest; this was considered one of the country's most enlightened periods.

HISTORICAL OVERVIEW

PRE-HISTORY 10,000 BC

Molvania emerged from the Iron Age when certain tribes in the north began hunting animals with weapons made entirely of unripe potatoes. Over the next 2,000 years the population dwindled to a mere 680 until legend has it that the warrior-king Zlag found a new, less starchy substance with which to construct utensils, thus dragging his country into the Cork Age.

CLASSICAL TIMES 50BC – ROMAN INVASION

Under the rule of Julius Caesar, most Roman expansion was perceived to be westward. But as General Maximus led his troops through Gaul, Iberia and Britain, another feared general, Hortensius Clarus, led his legions east through the Balkans until he got to the outpost known to the Romans as 'terra Mulvania – populus insanissimus'. His advance was stopped when, upon taking the city of Jraftrwok, he demanded the king's daughter as a concubine. She bravely slit his throat after he insisted she shave her armpits. When the retreating army brought back the general's decapitated body and a description of Molvanian women, Rome vowed never to set foot in Molvania again.

GOLDEN AGE AD720–988

While most of the western world went into decline during the Dark Ages, Molvania seemed to flourish during this period under the Gladbaag Dynasty. It was during this period that the greatest of all Molvanian poets, Ezrog, composed the epic tragi-comedy *Jzlakkensklowcza*, 20,000 verses based on the bawdy exploits of all the characters depicted in Tarot cards.

MODERN HISTORY

After centuries as a kingdom Molvania eventually declared itself a republic in 1834 and its leaders set about drawing up a **modern constitution**. The resulting document vested all executive powers in a Grand Wizard whose decisions could only be overruled during a full moon. Further attempts modernized the structure even further, forming the basis for Molvania's current democratic system of government. The first popularly elected Prime Minister was **Czez Vaduz** who ruled until his death in 1871. Such was this charismatic leader's popularity he was re-elected the following year.

The 20th century saw Molvania emerge as a semi-industrial powerhouse, one of the biggest parsnip- and liquorice-producing countries in the world. In 1940 the **Nazi Party** rose to power and Molvania was drawn into World War II as a German ally. Fifty years later many Molvanians are yet to fully accept this shameful period in their recent history, including the formation of a **secret military police** so brutal that occupying SS officers were afraid to have dealings with them. Sadly, even today there is a strong right-wing element in Molvanian politics, represented by the popular **Jsalter Party** (founded by popular nightclub singer turned statesman Igor Ztubalk, known to his fans as 'the Singing Neo-Nazi').

MOLVANIA'S POLITICAL STRUCTURE

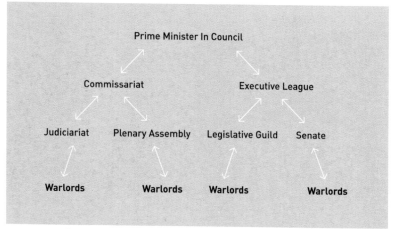

After the war Molvania found itself under Soviet control and endured many years of hardship and authoritarian rule. The turning point came in 1982 when the famous **Lutenblag Wall** collapsed, not due so much to democratic reform, but just shoddy construction. However, removal of this hated symbol of communist control led to Molvania holding its first democratic elections in

1983. These elections were won by a former military commander General Tzoric who scored a landslide victory – quite literally – when all members of the opposition party were buried by a freak landslide while out campaigning. Tzoric and his Rzelic Party ruled for the next decade before eventually being ousted in 1989 by the newly-formed **Peace Party**, who immediately declared war on Slovakia and Poland. A truce was eventually drawn up but, regrettably, Molvania entered a period of steep economic decline, culminating with the **Thirteen Year Strike** in which factory workers walked off the job for 4745 consecutive days over management plans to cut back on holiday bonuses.

In 1997 Molvania applied to become a member of the **European Union** but full membership has been slow in coming due, in part, to Molvania's refusal to allow **biological weapons** inspectors into the country.

Today Molvania is a country caught between the old world and the new, and the contrasts are many. It has provisional NATO membership and healthy IMF ratings, but is yet to declare **witch-burning** an indictable offence. Public services such as health care and education are woefully under-resourced yet there are nine government-funded TV networks. Despite these contradictions, or perhaps because of them, more and more people are visiting each year to experience the unique charm that is Molvania.

Prime Minister V. B. Tzoric congratulates the joint winners of the 1987 Young Despot of the Year Award (several weeks later, the one on the left killed the one on the right).

Molvania's much-loved Royal Family-in-exile.

THE FATHER OF MODERN MOLVANIA

You don't have to travel far in Molvania to come across the name Szlonko Busjbusj (1891–1948). Known as the Father of Modern Molvania, or more affectionately as 'Bu-Bu', this pioneering statesman has roads, bridges, statues, rivers and even a communicable disease named after him. And it's little wonder considering his numerous achievements as Prime Minister for several terms during the tumultuous 1930s. During that period Busjbusj managed to:

Szlonko Busjbusj ('Bu-Bu')

* de-regulate the country's tractor industry
* shorten the alphabet by 33 letters
* re-introduce the wheel
* reduce the maximum working weekend from 18 to 16 hours
* tie Molvania's currency (the *strubl*) to the Latvian *lit*
* establish the 'Balkan 7', a loose regional confederation of land-locked republics
* amend the Constitution to include a Bill of Rights guaranteeing all citizens the right to bear a grudge

But for all these extraordinary reforms 'Bu-Bu' is perhaps best remembered for his visionary economic guidance during the 1932 Great Depression. These were dark days for the world and Molvania; hyper-inflation forced people to walk around with wheelbarrows full of money simply in order to make basic grocery purchases. In a move that out-foxed the global financial community, Szlonko Busjbusj dealt with the problem by declaring wheelbarrows legal tender.

Even after retirement, Busjbusj continued to work tirelessly to unify the many opposing factions in Molvanian politics. He convened, and briefly led, a coalition called the United Party of Tyrants, Despots and Dictators. Unfortunately, as he grew old, his eyesight deteriorated badly – as did his adherence to human rights. Finally, in 1962 this 'blurred visionary' (as he was described in a UN War Crimes subpoena) died of natural causes – he was assassinated.

NATIONAL ANTHEM

Molvania's national anthem was chosen in 1987 as part of a competition, with the winning entry coming from an elderly local composer **V. J. Rzebren**. It is sung to the tune of '**Oh What a Feeling**' from *Flashdance*, with the third verse generally considered optional, as it is in contravention of EU laws against **racial vilification**.

	TRANSLATION
PRIJATI I-VSE PROST! ZVET BRAGK LE SOSED NE	We stand now vigorous and prospering
KJO RJOPAK TAVO GARBUS JKET SZOR	Forever united by our peoples
TEGUL DIRBA LIETVEJ TEGUL ZVUT STKER	Brothers within frontiers are we
OMOV DSKVI A TO JRE TA INACH MYSL	Supping upon the bounty of our home
PREJ LUK VDES PO JKADS KREMT VSE-TOI	Strife shall be banished and freedom reign
BJOR ESHTE QE DJESHMOR RTEH	Our women fertile as our seeping plains
EJUM JE TA ZVOR KRE ZSOVORTKIS	Let not the heroic past be forgotten
EJUM UND DAS SJORGEM FLAI	But the glorious future stand
VERBOT! SKUIG VAS-KLEM SVETHUM	Harmony and peace shall reign
STUMZ STUM PLAIS-DEIN STUMZ!	All invaders will be crushed
SEMIA TZASUMUS VO DIRBA PO	Crushed we sing now, crushed
OZIVLA KI VTOPIO BO-LE SKBRI	We shall drive the gypsy curse from our land

Molvania's biggest pop sensation, Olja, combines hot latin sounds with cold war rhetoric.

NATIONAL FLAG
The Molvanian 'trikolor' is unique for the fact it only has two colours. After the fall of the Iron Curtain, Molvania was the only ex-Soviet state to retain the hammer and sickle. So enamoured were they with the symbols of workers' unity, they added a third tool – the trowel.

GEOGRAPHY

Molvania was once described by a visiting writer as being at the 'crossroads of Eastern Europe' and – despite suspicions by some that he was simply being ironic – it retains a central place in European history. Geographically it is a diverse country, its southern regions largely made up of flat, **boggy marshland** and re-claimed swamps, while up in the north and west you'll find vast windswept plains.

The famous Tour dj Molvania or, as it's more commonly known, the 'EPO Classic'.

There are, of course, mountains in the far south-east of the country; the world-renowned **Postenwalj Ranges** through which the popular Tour dj Molvania bicycle race passes each year. During the winter months these hills become a Mecca for skiers although, at just over 700m, the snow cover can become a little **desert-like**, hence the description 'Mecca'.

Two main waterways cross the country: the mighty River Uze that snakes through the centre of the country all the way west until it crosses the border into Germany (where it's known as the '**Saxony Sewer**'); and the smaller, but no less impressive, River Fiztula in the country's south.

Much of the central valley region was arid and bare but thanks to copious amounts of fertilizer, coupled with the Molvanian Government's open-door approach to **genetically-modified crops**, local farmers have been able to produce ample supplies of maize, corn, beetroot and a peculiar potato-like hybrid EU scientists are yet to officially classify as a food-stuff.

Molvania prides itself as an environmentally conscious nation, and all its **waste** is either sorted and re-cycled, or dumped over the border in Slovakia. The average precipitation is 67cm per year, which falls as mainly snow, sleet or acid rain.

Geographically, Molvania is a land of contrasts – from its rocky, semi-barren hills to its rocky, semi-barren plains.

MOLVANÎA

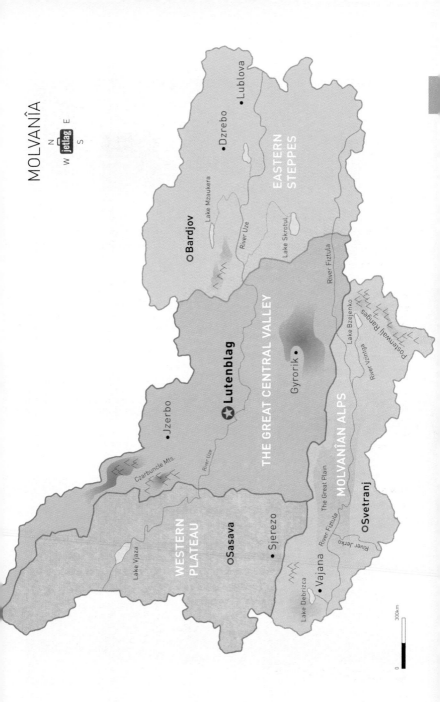

W **jetlag** E
N
S

WESTERN PLATEAU
Lake Vjaza
○Sasava
• Sjerezo
Czarbuncle Mts.
Lake Debrizca
• Vajana

THE GREAT CENTRAL VALLEY
• Jzerbo
★ **Lutenblag**
River Uze
Gyrorik •

MOLVANÎAN ALPS
The Great Plain
River Fiztula
River Jerko
○Svetranj
River Vzmga
Lake Bzejenko
Postemwalj Ranges

EASTERN STEPPES
Lake Mzaukera
• Dzrebo
• Lublova
River Uze
Lake Skrotul
River Fiztula

○Bardjov

0   300km

THE PEOPLE

In AD 60 the Roman historian **Tacitus** described the Molvanian people thus:

> *They are short and dark of appearance, not given to hard work or creative thinking. In fact, you would have to travel many miles to find a more argumentative, unruly, uncultured tribe of hunter-gatherers in all of the Empire...*

Even today Molvanians are often misrepresented as being surly, short-tempered and prone to violence, but of course this only represents one part of the picture. Deep down the Molvanian people are fun-loving folk with that typically warm **Slavic sense of humour**. There are aspects of their behaviour that may take a little getting used to – such as their **phone manner**, in which brusqueness is considered a virtue. But hospitality is a key part of Molvanian culture and there's an old saying *zva grek inst ur plebum szunj* ('better that a stranger be across thy door than a friend upon the road thereon'), which, while perhaps losing a little in the translation, pretty much sums up the Molvanian's carefree attitude to life.

Whilst culturally diverse, the Molvanian population is made up of three major ethnic groups: the **Bulgs** (68%), who live predominantly in the centre and south; the **Hungars** (29%), who inhabit the northern cities; and the **Molvs** (3%), who can be found mainly in prison.

GYPSIES

Some European countries are marred by racial disharmony between permanent residents and their itinerant **gypsy** population. Molvania prides itself on the fact this is not a problem as most of its gypsies have been successfully driven abroad or **incarcerated**.

CUSTOMS

Molvanians are not, as a rule, a particularly formal people, however there are **basic rules** governing social contact that are worth adhering to. Upon meeting someone in the street, shake their hand and bow slightly unless the person is older in which case simply bow and clip the heels, remembering that a handshake in such circumstances would cause enormous **offence**, as would clipping the heels in the presence of a married woman or member of the clergy. If invited into someone's home, remember to always remove your shoes in the entrance as a sign of respect, and to give yourself something with which to hit the family pet should it attack. Once inside, take care to avoid **blowing your nose** (or anyone else's for that matter) within sight of the kitchen. It's also appropriate to bring a small gift, be it flowers, fruit, firearms, or – if there are children – cigarettes. It's polite to wait until your host (the *purv*) indicates where to sit before being seated. If sitting on traditional *fjukazl* matting, women are advised to sit with their legs together, especially if seated opposite the *purv*.

Traveller's Tip

First time visitors to Molvania are often struck by the rather direct manner in which locals treat each other, whether in shops, whilst driving or simply walking down the street. Raised voices and wild gesticulations are common and – to an outsider – it would appear no-one seems to particularly like each other. The truth is that Molvanians are simply a very forthright people, not overly concerned with the niceties of human interaction. Waving a fist at another driver or spitting on a family member is all part of daily life for these easy-going folk. Of course, for a new arrival it takes a bit of time to work out how you should behave in return – the precise degree of brusqueness required, for example, to catch the attention of a waiter. If you are too meek he will ignore you. If you are too aggressive he may produce a concealed weapon. My advice is to err on the courteous side. Wherever possible say 'brobra' ('thank you') to your concierge and 'vriszi' ('please') to the waiter. Tell your taxi driver his car is clean (there's actually no Molvanian phrase for this situation but you can always use hand signals). In short, try a little courtesy and see how far you get.

PLANTS & ANIMALS

Once cloaked in dense forest, much of Molvania is now made up of **barren plains**. Legend has it that St Fyodor was responsible for ridding the country of its trees but the arrival of **chainsaws** in the 1950s certainly sped up the process. Molvania grows much of the world's supply of gherkin and silverbeet, as well as *hvobecz*, a small, bitter nut often used in the centre of golf balls. In terms of fauna, the country boasts more rodents per square kilometre than anywhere else in the world. Larger species include bears, deer, lynx, wild boar and the famed **Molvanian Sneezing Hound**.

The fzipdat or serrated thistle is the floral emblem of Molvania, a sharply thorned cactus traditionally thrown at Molvanian brides. Its leaves have an astringent, bitter taste, making it a popular ingredient in local dishes.

The pig is generally considered the symbol of Molvania. Believed to be sacred by many, these animals may only be slaughtered Monday to Saturday. Pigs are widely used throughout the country for meat, milk and – in remote areas – companionship.

SPORTS

Like so many Western European nations, Molvania is football mad. Sadly, their national team has had little in the way of international success, especially since the introduction of random drug-testing. Molvania's highest-profile player would without doubt be **Viordar Czervkle** (or 'Cze' as he is affectionately known) and everywhere you will see his name on T-shirts and posters. To the dismay of most local fans Cze no longer plays at a professional level due to a serious injury; he was banned for **head-butting** a Croatian referee during an international friendly in 1996.

Lutenblag Stadium (the *Lutenstaad*) was built in 1985 in anticipation of Molvania being successful with its plans to host the 1994 World Cup. Sadly their bid failed and much of the ground has since fallen into disrepair. Designed to hold 80,000 spectators it is now used largely for rock concerts and **public hangings**.

Interblag F.C., also known as 'The Invincibles', shortly before their 1995 semi-final defeat. (Viordar Czervkle can be seen back row, second from right)

The Lutenblag Stadium (the Lutenstaad)

Home-Grown Hero!

Molvania's most famous sporting hero, pentathlete Hzerge Voldarj, was born in Sasava and trained at the Institut Medekina Anabolika in Lutenblag before being chosen to represent his country in the 1982 winter Olympics in Modern Biathlon. Tragically, whilst in the lead, he was disqualified on a technicality during the shooting event when, instead of hitting the target, he instinctively turned and took aim at a passing rabbit. Voldarj subsequently retired from international competition and now hosts his own sports-based TV quiz show 'Ask Hzerge'.

Unique to Molvania is the game of **Plutto**, which has been described as a sort of cross between lacrosse and polo played on a donkey. These animals are specially bred for this sport, with those bearing larger ears highly sought-after. On most Saturday afternoons local parks and ovals echo to the sound of spectators crying *'bzoukal! bzoukal!'* (literally 'slash his throat!') as their heroes fight it out.

The other great sporting passion in Molvania is, of course, hunting and most children learn to shoot from a very early age. **Wild boar** are perhaps the most popular quarry, and the hunting season lasts from mid-October until whenever people have run out of **ammunition**. Other targets include ducks, geese, foxes, wild bears, road signs and rabbits, although visitors should be reminded that these can only be hunted by a person holding a valid **shooting licence** or related to someone who does.

An Olympic Moment...

Molvania has had a long and proud Olympic history, picking up medals in both summer and winter games. During the communist era the country held the record for producing the greatest number of defecting athletes, the highpoint being the 1976 Montreal Games during which the entire team attempted to jump ship, entering the stadium under a white flag.

The Molvanian Tennis Open is one of the few ATP events played on a combination of clay and grass.

Molvania's greatest living Plutto champion on his prized steed, Klodd.

RELIGION

Molvanians are a deeply religious people and most belong to a church, or are supported by one. The most dominant religion is **Baltic Orthodox**, a local form of worship very similar to Catholicism (except that Catholics long ago dismissed the concept of the world being flat). Baltic Orthodox congregations may also smoke in church. This religion dates back thousands of years and local believers will proudly tell you that one of the two robbers crucified next to Christ was in fact from Molvania.

Many devout practitioners will regularly follow the pilgrim trail that leads to the holy shrine of **St Ulgmat** in Jzerbo. It was here, back in 1534, that two shepherds on their way home from a local hostelry claimed to have seen a vision hovering in the field ahead. So intense was the power of this **apparition** that both men fell into a deep sleep, waking the next morning with severe headaches and blurred vision.

If invited to a Molvanian church remember that **appropriate clothing** is required; women should wear a dress and possibly a hat, and men should make sure at least one of their shirt buttons is done up.

In **Holy Week**, from Palm Sunday to Easter, Molvanian families may not eat meat, and from Good Friday married couples will often abstain from domestic violence.

Here Comes the Bride...!

Molvanian weddings are events of enormous social significance and as such are surrounded by elaborate ritual. Traditionally the celebrations begin with the bride and groom fasting for 24 hours. After this time the woman is forbidden from leaving the house while her future husband goes out drinking. As the big day approaches the bride is bathed in scented oils, her bodily hair is completely waxed off* and she is sumptuously dressed. The wedding ceremony itself is long and joyous, followed by much feasting and drinking – after which the happy couple are led into separate rooms to consummate their union.

* *In areas of northern Molvania this part of the process can often take several days.*

St Fyodor – Patron Saint of Molvania (AD1507–1563)

St Fyodor was born in 1507 to a family of wealthy Molvanian landowners. At the age of just four he amazed church elders by drinking an entire vat of **communion wine**. It was a religious feat he was to repeat many times later in life. From his mother Fyodor inherited a quiet manner and pious devotion to God. From his father he inherited gout. Fyodor's first period of devotion began when, as a 10-year-old, he was sent to help his family run their farm but refused to take part, saying it was God's will that he remain inside to pray and meditate. Such was his devotion to this task that the young man would only come out for meals and public holidays. During these periods he would often fast for up to three hours at a time, dedicating his discomfort to the Lord.

Fyodor was a man of many contradictions. When his father's house burnt down, he remarked that he did not mind as material belongings meant nothing to him. Yet a few weeks later he almost clubbed a man to death for stealing his **lute** in what theologians believe must have been a fit of religious fervour.

A great friend of the poor, Fyodor took particular interest in young single women and could often be seen visiting their homes at all hours of the day and night, armed only with a Bible and a bottle of **sacramental red**. Here he would preach the Gospel and offer to lay hands on those who kneeled before him.

Such was St Fyodor's devotion to the Lord that, at the age of 21, he announced that he'd been called to give up all movement. As part of this devotion he would sit by the fire in quiet contemplation for months on end, taking no nourishment save three meals a day plus snacks. At other times he would disappear for long periods without explanation, returning from his devotions with **slurred speech** and unsteady gait – a sign, he claimed, that the Holy Spirit was dwelling within.

At the age of 56 and weighing over 100kg he was arrested by **Protestant militiamen** who demanded he denounce his faith or be killed. Fyodor refused, saying calmly that the Lord would protect him. At this point he was tied to a tree, whipped, shot with arrows and beheaded. His last words were 'copra sanctum' ('holy shit').

St Fyodor was beatified by Pope Paul in 1617, canonized by Pope Gregory XV in 1623 and featured posthumously on an episode of Molvania's '**This is Your Life**' in 1982.

Relics of his underpants can be found at the Chapel of St Fyodor in Lutenblag.

– from *Lives of the Saints* (Vatican University Press)

LANGUAGE

Molvanian is a difficult language to speak, let alone master. There are **four genders**: male, female, neutral, and the collective noun for cheeses, which occupies a nominative sub-section of its very own. The language also contains numerous **irregular verbs**, archaic phrases, words of multiple meaning and several phonetic sounds linguists suspect could represent either a rare dialect or merely peasants clearing their throat. This, coupled with a record number of **silent letters**, makes fluency a major challenge. You can, as some visitors have experimented with, simply try adding the letter 'j' or 'z' randomly to any word – but this will only get you so far.

Perhaps a better option is to memorise a few of our 'Useful Phrases' contained opposite. Remember, too, that the syntactical structure of written Molvanian can be rather complex, with writers routinely using the **triple negative**. Hence,

> 'Can I drink the water? '
> becomes '*Erkjo ne szlepp statsik ne var ne vladrobzko ne* '
> (literally, 'is it not that the water is not not undrinkable?')

Fortunately, conversational Molvanian for the native speaker is a little less formal, and a native speaker wanting to know

> 'Can I drink the water? '
> would only have to say '*Virkum stas*?'
> (while clutching their stomach in a gesture of gastric distress).

For those keen to learn Molvanian there is a private school in Lutenblag that offers an intensive summer course. For some, this is a marvellous way of immersing themselves in the culture and traditions of Molvania. For most, it is a complete **waste of time**. Please note, several former pupils have reported that the teacher, a Mr Hzocbeter, can be a little on the aggressive side, especially when it comes to irregular verbs.

The Lutenblag Private Language Academy (the Linguistikprivatakademikalutnblaag*)*

USEFUL PHRASES

COMMON EXPRESSIONS

Zlkavszka	Hello
Grovzsgo	Goodbye
Vrizsi	Please
Brobra	Thank you
Wakuz Dro Brugka Spazibo	Good luck *(literally 'May God send you a sturdy donkey')*
Sprufki Doh Craszko?	What is that smell?
Dyuszkiya trappokski drovko?	Does it always rain this much?
Kyunkasko sbazko byusba?	Where is the toilet paper?
Togurfga trakij sdonchskia?	What happened to your teeth?

LESS COMMON EXPRESSIONS

Frijyhadsgo drof, huftrawxzkio	More food, inn-keeper.
Ok hyrafrpiki kidriki	What beautiful children!

VERY RARE EXPRESSIONS

Krokystrokiskiaskya	See you again soon.

Tongue-Twisting...!
The US State Department ranks languages by the time it takes their operatives and trainees to learn them. Spanish is listed at five months while North Korean and Arabic take 24. Molvanian is officially classified as 16 years and hence is considered at the difficult end of the spectrum. The official State Department guide lists several reasons for this, including the ability for the same word to be both complimentary and insulting depending on the key in which it is vocalised.

HEALTH ALERT!
DUE TO THE ABUNDANCE OF GUTTURAL PHONETIC SOUNDS FOUND IN THE SPOKEN LANGUAGE, NON-NATIVE MOLVANIAN SPEAKERS ARE WARNED ABOUT THE RISK OF LARYNGEAL DAMAGE THAT CAN ARISE FROM ATTEMPTING ANYTHING MORE THAN A FEW SHORT PHRASES.

FOOD & DRINK

Molvanians love eating out – preferably in France or Germany – but those dining within the borders of this unique country will find it a vibrant and exciting **culinary experience**.

Only in Molvania can one sample traditional fare such as *horsflab* (the local **pickled meat** delicacy) washed down with a glass of *zeerstum*, a liqueur one reader described as tasting like 'a mixture of vodka and Avgas' – quite understandable as both are common ingredients.

Horsflab *is a popular local delicacy.*

Most Molvanians also have a sweet tooth – often the only one left after a lifetime of **overly sweetened food** – and national desserts here are a gastronome's delight, with a surprisingly wide variety given that so many of them are based on the **parsnip**.

American-style coffee shops are common throughout the country but, of course, old habits die hard and most mornings around 11.00am you'll see many elderly Molvanians, propped up in a *zvadovar* bar, drinking cups of this heavily-sugared **chicory extract** through cork filters.

Traveller's Tip

Zvadovar *cafes are a great way to soak in the atmosphere, but remember that sitting at a table outside can be costly. A better idea is to join the locals standing up inside the cafe, although be warned – you will be charged extra if your elbow comes into contact with any part of the bar surface area.*

Molvanian wines are exported all over the world – and for good reason. No-one at home is prepared to drink them.

Those in need of a fast-food fix will notice several Burger Kings, McDonalds and KFC stores have opened up in the main centres, though not without a fight from many local groups who opposed the arrival of such **US-based restaurant chains**. In the end a compromise was reached and all products sold at these outlets must contain 12% local **cabbage**, except for the milkshakes, which require just 10%. There are also home-grown fast-food franchises such as the popular **Zitz Pizza** restaurants, where the owners advertise an attractive 'second helpings are free' policy, safe in the knowledge this offer will rarely be taken up.

As a rule, eating out in Molvania is quite cheap, especially compared to other parts of Europe, but take care to check the menu prices for **added extras** such as a 10% service fee (20% if you want cutlery), which can bump the cost up. In some of the larger cities you may also be expected to pay extra for a waiter with a moustache.

Alcohol can easily be purchased throughout Molvania in most bars, restaurants, cafes, supermarkets and churches.

The Local Drop...
One of the most popular drinks in Molvania is *turpz*, a white wine flavoured with oak resin. This fruity drop is an acquired taste, but once tasted, it's hard to give up, due in part to the fact that it contains nicotine.

Fishy Business!
One of the most sought-after delicacies in Molvania is *ovza*, the local caviar made from the eggs of freshwater carp. Slightly sour with a bitter aftertaste, the fish roe is generally salted, boiled, tenderized and then preserved in oil for several years before being served as a decorative garnish.

Despite being a land-locked country, Molvanians love their seafood.
Here a fisherman from Lake Vjaza checks his catch for mercury levels.

MUSIC

FOLK

Molvania has a rich musical heritage, the origins of which stretch back to the Middle Ages when **shepherds** would carry a *kvkadra* (a simple brass horn used to drive away wolves). Unfortunately this instrument had a similar effect on audiences and, during the 16th century, it was modified into what we now call a *zjardrill* (a sort of goat-skin bagpipe played by pumping the bellows with one's left elbow whilst moving a series of valves and reeds up and down a finger board). For all this **technical complexity**, the *zjardrill* was only capable of producing three notes, but despite this limitation a rich folk tradition soon developed around it. Even today these instruments can still be heard, especially in outlying areas where people gather to enjoy **traditional dances** such as the *mzazeruk* (in which a trio of young women perform an **energetic jig** whilst a circle of men attempt to fondle them).

CLASSICAL

Classical music has also played a large part in Molvania's cultural history and the great **Tzozar Czevkel** (1772–1821) is still recognized as one of the most prolific composers of his time. Born in Gyorik just a few years after Beethoven, this Molvanian maestro shared a lot with his German contemporary. Both men battled poverty and, like Beethoven, Czevkel was deaf – or more accurately, **tone-deaf** – but despite these difficulties he produced an enormous body of work encompassing chamber and orchestral music, masses and dances. His *Concerto for Tuba and Triangle in E flat minor* remains one of the most distinctive, if rarely-performed, works in symphonic history.

On Air! Although there is no FM-band, pop music can be heard on the AM-band or the more popular CB-band.

The other great figure of Molvanian classical music was **Azmon Dirj** (1856–1879) who is generally known as 'the father of the semi-quaver'. Dirj composed several operas that perfectly captured the essential joy, dignity and power of the human condition. That he was able to do this within the musical framework of the **polka** says much for the depth of his talent. Many of Dirj's works are still performed by the world-renowned Molvanian Opera Company. This neoclassical ensemble performs nightly at the **Lutenblag State Theatre** where headphones can be hired to provide simultaneous translation into English. Alternatively, they can simply be used to block out the music.

CHORAL

No visit to this part of the world would be complete without experiencing the haunting harmonies of the **Molvanian Boys Choir**. Despite recent negative publicity surrounding their choirmaster's 'extra-curricular' activities (all charges were actually dismissed by a Swiss court), the young vocalists continue to delight. Here's a tip – catch them now before proposed **anti-castration** laws are formally passed.

Spatzal!

Two girls, one guy and a transvestite make up Molvania's most successful pop music act, the award-winning Spatzal!, who made it to fifth place in the 1998 Eurovision Song Contest with their catchy dance tune '*Vlarsh ei Czolom*' ('Your Boogy I am Shaking'). Sadly, the group split up in 2001 (bass player Vron Gzapaov reportedly has a solo album in the works) but such was their influence that there are numerous Spatzal! tribute bands still touring the Baltic region.

Following the success of their previous L.P.s **Im' Ready From Yuo!**' *(1993) and* **Hey Beutifulls!**' *(1994), Spatzal's* **Let's Rock!**' *(1996) proved to be an historic album, described by* Rolling Stone *as Molvania's first ever correctly-spelt English language release.*

THEATRE, ART & LITERATURE

In the 1920s Molvania was the theatrical capital of Europe, and its most famous practitioner was the Marxist poet and playwright **Jurzse Vepcojat** (1897–1946). Vepcojat revolutionised the **dramatic arts** by inventing a new form of theatre in which the writer deliberately set out to alienate his audience – a philosophy he pursued with considerable success, and one that has influenced all Molvanian playwrights since.

Even today Vepcojat's plays can clear a packed opening night theatre audience within minutes.

Molvania has many outstanding works of art, most of them plundered from Italy during the 17th century wars. As far as home-grown talent goes, one need look no further than Molvania's most famous artist, the enigmatic **Jzacol Rebljeten** (1583–1611). Rebljeten was a dedicated craftsman who had a detailed knowledge of anatomy that came from hours spent dissecting corpses. Interestingly, this knowledge proved of little direct benefit to his art as he only ever painted landscapes, but Rebljeten still managed to produce some of the most important works ever to come out of central Europe. A strong feature of his painting was the way he **deliberately distorted** the proportions of his subjects in what many scholars believe was an early attempt to abandon **Naturalism** in favour of the Mannerist style. Others have suggested he just wasn't very good at drawing, but whatever the case, Rebljeten's works are proudly displayed in galleries throughout Molvania.

One of the strongest movements in Molvanian art was pioneered by a group of people called the *Sverkj Krempzes* ('Courtroom Artists'), who emerged during the 20th century when local Mafia figures would commission them to capture on canvas their major courtroom appearances.

With a long and rich history of literature it's hard to pick any one author who best typifies Molvanian writing. Many would argue it is the acclaimed nationalist **Bratislav Demkjo** (1734–1789), a peasant by birth, who wrote plays, novels and satiric verse. His most famous work was the **epic poem** *Gorzenmko ur Turj* ('My Beating Heart'), 12 volumes of densely allegorical, highly-stylised verse depicting the fortunes of a working class Molvanian family. It has been described by scholars as one of the most significant works never read.

HUMOUR
Molvanians are often described as dour, humourless people, but the truth is they enjoy a laugh as much as the next Eastern European. Molvanian comedy can, however, take a little getting used to. A typical joke would be: **'A man is shooting deer in the woods when he comes across a chest full of gold coins. "This must belong to someone very wealthy" he thinks and decides to sit in wait for the owner to return so he can rob him of the wealth!'** *(The joke, of course, being that he could have just taken the coins, thus avoiding the need for a lengthy wait and subsequent criminal act.)*

Molvanians love a laugh – preferably at someone else's expense.

NEWSPAPERS, FILM & VIDEO

There is one English-language newspaper published in Molvania, the tourist-oriented *Lutenblag Today*. However, this comes out monthly, with the result that some of its listings may be out of date.

Molvanians are avid film-goers and there are **numerous cinemas** throughout the country showing a wide range of movies, from Hollywood blockbusters through to independent releases from local directors such as **Jzan Zetwiski**. Widely regarded as a cinematic auteur, Zetwiski describes his films as 'modern fables, exploring the themes of morality and beauty in a random universe'. Others call them '**cheap Euro porn**', which only serves to highlight the multi-layered brilliance of this young visionary's work.

If you want to see a film in Molvania remember that most of them are dubbed or sub-titled, sometimes both. It's worth avoiding dubbed films as all character's voices seem to be supplied by the same two actors, both men, one of whom has a **noticeable stutter**.

For those after in-house movie viewing there are plenty of video hire outlets to be found, the only drawback being that Molvania firmly embraced the Beta system of video recorder in the 1980s, declaring it 'the way of the future'. Fortunately, **Beta video** players are also available for hire, as are eight-track audio tape players and 'Space Invaders' consoles.

There is a newly opened multiplex in Lutenblag featuring eight screens, although at the time of writing it only had the one projector.

TV

Molvanian TV is not good. There are three state run channels: Telemolva 1, Telemolva 2 and the premium network **Telemolva Plus**, which is in colour.

All channels feature a mixture of tawdry Slovakian soaps, football matches, badly dubbed films and a home-produced news program `Molva Tuja!`, that features information about which members of the government have been arrested that day.

Whilst very little programming is **broadcast in English** it is still possible for visitors stuck in a hotel room to glean a few cultural insights by tuning in. A typical day's viewing looks like this:

6.30am Good Morning Molvania!
(including news, views and death notices).

8.30am Ctvrtek Listek.
Slovakian drama series. Putlo realizes the mule may be lying. Stand-over man Standova makes Ziva an offer he can't understand.

10.30am Station closed
for technical repairs.

3pm Nejbors (Neighbours).
Australian drama series featuring sunburnt teenagers. Sparks fly when Zarlin (Charlene) shows Zcott (Scott) her *tulbok* (toolbox).

3.30pm Molvanian Family Feud.
Two families, a long-standing grudge and numerous concealed weapons make this the country's most popular game show.

5pm Dj Bradj Bunj (The Brady Bunch).
Re-make of US comedy. A widower with three boys marries a widow with three liquor licences. Much mirth ensues. (Repeat)

7pm Telenewz. All the latest from the live eye news centre in Lutenblag.

7.30pm Molva Tuja!
In depth current affairs program (features Lotto Draw 4113)

8.30pm Marszalkowska.
Medico-legal police drama. Tempers fray when Zep, Jerv, Marta, Theodor and Bruc realize there are too many of them working on the case.

9.30pm The Late Show with Brashko Vedev.
Music, laughter and chat from Molvania's Mr Entertainment. Tonight's guests include local soccer legend Viordar Czervkle and comedy duo 'Vatsak'. Featuring Brashko's 'Wheel of Torture'.

11.30pm Epiloj. Fr. Jzerco Mzemet (below) offers a prayer to end the day.

11.32pm All night Adult Movie marathon.
Lesbian Nurses at Home (XXX) and more!!!

WHEN TO GO

Depending on what you want from your trip, any time can be good to visit Molvania. As a general rule, spring and autumn tend to be wet, winter is **bitterly cold** and in the summer the **heat can be oppressive**. The busiest season is, naturally, July when much of the country is deluged by Slovenian tour buses. Those wanting a quieter, less-crowded experience might consider visiting in the 'off-season' periods such as winter or during the **Lutenblag Jazz Festival**. Many travellers find it useful planning their trip to coincide with one of the many public holidays or feast days Molvanians love to celebrate. Some of the major ones include:

CALENDAR OF EVENTS

*2 FEBRUARY	**St Fyodor's Day**. The birth-date of Molvania's patron saint is marked by a public holiday featuring parades, masses and a huge international arms fair.
*MARCH	Visit the picturesque hillside town of Lublova for the traditional **Running of the Bulls** in which a frightened herd of cattle flee from a group of heavily-armed young men. A large BBQ feast follows.
*MARCH/APRIL	**Easter** is a major event in Molvania and in every town and village locals will dress up, often in traditional costume, and celebrate the resurrection with music, dancing and each others' wives.
*APRIL	In most towns the festival of **Spiegleglaz** traditionally involves villagers dancing and singing as they welcome in the spring: unfortunately the ceremony is often cancelled due to rain.
*1 MAY	Opening of the **hunting season** which runs until 30 April. Shooting is a very popular pastime in Molvania with duck, quail and pheasant all on the endangered list.
*JUNE	The **Lutenblag Film Festival** invites filmmakers from all over Europe, but generally only receives acceptances from Bulgaria and Romania.
*6, 7 or 14 JULY	Molvania's **National Day of Unity** celebrates the anniversary of the country coming together as a unified nation-state. Unfortunately there's still some disagreement over precisely what date this event should be celebrated on.
*AUGUST	The Molvanian **Military Tattoo** is staged each year in the grounds of the Lutenblag Palace. Highlights include a performance by the famous Royal Skidding Horses whose 'slide and dismount' demonstration is a real crowd-pleaser, especially when the 'screen' comes out.
*OCTOBER	For those staying in Lutenblag this is the big one – **Swinefest** (starting the last Sunday of October, ending when the blood congeals).
*DECEMBER	**Christmas** in Molvania is celebrated on 27 December, a date that gives locals the opportunity to cross the border to take advantage of cheap gift-buying sprees at Boxing Day sales abroad.

CRIME

Even in a relatively safe country like Molvania, travellers must still be aware that the possibility of theft or violence exists. **Pickpockets** are active around many of the **major railway stations** and you should keep a close eye on your belongings. If something does go missing the best thing to do is look for a *Guarjda Civilje*. Chances are he will be the person who stole it.

Another area worth avoiding is the Sklertzen precinct of inner-city Lutenblag, where elements of the Molvanian Mafia are known to operate. At night this becomes a **red-light district**, featuring seedy strip joints where local businessmen can be seen stuffing US dollars into the garter belts of some of the oldest sex workers in the Balkans.

Should you find it necessary to report a crime, remember there are 17 different branches of Molvanian *polizi*, each with their own specific area of responsibility. For example, a motor vehicle accident requires the *Polizi Autzo* (tel 133), while a **violent crime** calls for the *Polizi Hzuomo* (tel 128). In the unlikely event you suffer an act of **international piracy**, the *Polizi Aquza* (tel 142) are the ones to call.

Though generally a tolerant organization, Molvania's police will not hesitate to issue fines for misdemeanours such as speeding and public drunkenness, regardless of whether the offender is a local or a tourist. Jail terms may result from more serious breaches of the law such as assault, theft or breast-feeding in public.

Philippe Miseree writes...

" *It's pathetic, tourists complaining about pickpockets and worrying that they might get mugged if they go into a certain section of town. For me, being the victim of minor crime is an essential part of the overall travel experience. Once, in a seedy*

Lutenblag hotel room, I woke to discover that thieves had stolen my wallet, camera and a kidney – it was a trip I will never forget! "

P.M.

Sadly, underworld influences have taken over even the egg trade.

WOMEN TRAVELLERS

Women travelling alone through Molvania should expect few problems aside from the usual **assault,** armed robbery and stalking that one sees in most Eastern European countries. A wedding ring (worn on the left hand) has one advantage in that it may help prevent you becoming the subject of amorous advances. On the downside, it will make you a certain target for gypsy thieves.

DISABLED TRAVELLERS

Molvania prides itself on its attitudes to the disabled and in 1985 it passed legislation allowing them to **beg** without a permit.

GAY TRAVELLERS

Although conservative, Molvanians have taken great steps forward over recent years and in many parts of the country it is no longer compulsory for men to grow a moustache. Some of the bigger cities even permit **cologne**. Of course, visitors are officially free to do as they wish, although one has to weigh up the right to display open affection with the probability of being publicly beaten.

Gay travellers are welcome in most parts of Molvania but care should be taken not to stand out.

Fakin' It !
Like many Eastern European countries, Molvanian currency has its fair share of forgeries and visitors should be alert to avoid getting ripped off by counterfeit notes. When passed a Molvanian strubl, be on the look out for poor quality paper, smudged ink and spelling errors; notes displaying these features are likely to be authentic.

USEFUL FACTS

ELECTRICITY

Supply to all but the most outlying areas of Molvania is now fairly reliable; however, the electrical current is a rather unusual 37 volts, having been chosen using numerology charts. If you plan on using appliances manufactured outside Molvania a transformer will be required.

Note: Make sure the appliance is well earthed and there are no flammable liquids within 3m.

CURRENCY

1 strubl (♻1) = 100 qunts (100q)

In times of war or economic crisis garlic is often accepted as legal tender. Since deregulation the strubl has had a rocky ride on international markets and has been significantly devalued in recent years, but with the official inflation rate now well under 28% some stability has been restored.

During times of severe economic recession garlic may be accepted as legal tender.

CREEPY-CRAWLIES

Insect repellent is a must, preferably extra-strength, to cope with Molvania's range of insect life: mosquitoes (January—March), wasps (February—May), midges (April—August), earwigs (August—October) and leeches (year-round).

PHOTOGRAPHY

With picturesque villages and stunning scenery Molvania is a great place for shutter-bugs. In general, people are pleased to be photographed, but please ask first.

Note: Never photograph gypsies without explicit permission and a clear escape route.

PASSPORTS

Remember, a valid passport is required at all border crossings and certain undesirable visitors may be refused entry, such as convicted felons, those with links to a terrorist organization or vegetarians.

HOW TO GET THERE
Air The national airline of Molvania is Aeromolv, the subject of much press coverage back in 2000 when its pilots went on strike in protest over government plans to prohibit them drinking alcohol within two hours of a flight. Aeromolv's fleet consists mainly of older B-717 aircraft; passengers board through the nosewheel hatch. There are also several 'no-frills' carriers for those prepared to travel without the luxury of in-flight dining or navigation equipment.

Aeromolv's Chief Pilot, Capt. Jelso Vrboska, completes pre-flight safety checks.

Bus Most major European cities have bus routes that take in Lutenblag and other provincial cities. Government-run companies are generally the best and most reliable. Avoid cut-price private transport operators in places like Slovenia and Poland as their 'budget' services will often involve crossing the border inside a sealed shipping container.

HOW TO GET AWAY
The departure tax is ∫ 3000 – one of the highest in Europe, but most visitors agree it's well worth the price. You'll also have to fill out a Departure Card. Many readers have pointed out the intrusive nature of the last few questions, involving sexual contacts and phone numbers.

Note: Answering is not obligatory, but much appreciated by the immigration officials.

HOW TO GET AROUND
Car is the most popular form of transport; however, many Molvanian roads struggle to cope with the traffic demands placed upon them. Lutenblag and Svetranj are linked by one of the only cobblestone autobahns in all of Europe. Remember that Molvanians drive on the right, although around Christmas and national holidays this rule can get a little blurred. Cars must still give way to tractors, and children under 12 years of age must ride in the back seat. (The same rule applies to livestock.) In major towns parking spaces are marked with a blue line and a sign denoting time restrictions. 'No Parking' areas are marked by a sign with a red circle around a skull and crossbones symbol.

CUSTOMS & DUTIES

Strict rules govern what may and may not be brought into Molvania. Visitors are permitted to carry a maximum of 2500 cigarettes for each adult (children can carry 1500). There are technically **no limits** on the amount of alcohol one may bring in to the country, but customs inspectors will often demand you open a bottle so they can test its contents before letting you through. As for exporting alcohol, there are no restrictions on the amount of Molvanian wine that may be taken out of the country – in fact, the government offers **cash incentives** for those prepared to take two dozen bottles or more.

HOSPITALS & PHARMACIES

Gone are the days when it was necessary for visitors to come equipped with personal **first-aid kits** and their own blood supplies.* Pharmacies exist in most major cities and can prescribe drugs for common complaints (diarrhoea, sore throat, syphillus) and also sell Immodium, Tampax, Aspirin and a locally manufactured **contraceptive pill** so effective that one dose will rule out the possibility of falling pregnant for the next five years. In outlying areas of the country, medical supplies can generally be obtained from the local stock agent, although visitors should be warned against purchasing unusually **cheap medications** bearing the phrase 'zve crojezn ub' ('animal use only').

   Clinics and doctors' surgeries are also widespread throughout Molvania and most of the major cities have at least one hospital. The **Lutenblag Public Hospital** not only provides a full range of out-patient facilities, it is one of the few medical centres in Europe to offer a 24-hour autopsy service.

REST ROOMS

Public rest rooms (*urinjaztkis*) are more common and cleaner than they used to be in Molvania. You'll generally have to pay ⌇40–50 to an attendant who will, in return, hand you some toilet paper and a form to sign indemnifying the owners for any long-term physical or psychological damage resulting from your visit. Of course, in outlying areas public toilets are all but **non-existent** and locals 'caught short' will simply use a tree, stone fence or civic monument.

Molvanian Rest Room Signs

HOT & COLD WATER

Molvanian plumbing can be a little complicated, especially as it changes depending on which part of the country you are in. In the capital Lutenblag and most western cities you'll find the hot water tap on your left and cold on your right, with both being turned on in a **counter-clockwise** direction. However, in the east and some mountainous regions of the south this layout is reversed and the taps are operated by a lever located to the left of the hot tap or right of the cold, depending on which way you're facing.

* Although it still wouldn't hurt.

DRINKING WATER

Despite recent improvements in Molvania's water supply system, concerns still exist over the quality and safety of most tap water. Boiling the water before you drink it will get rid of most **bacterial contamination**, but the heavier than recommended lead levels still pose health risks (see the section on 'Molvania's Royal Family'). Bottled water is readily available and a sensible alternative.

One glass of Molvanian tap water contains 80% of your annual requirements of trace metals and e-coli.

TIPPING

In Molvania it is not generally necessary to tip, unless of course you want something done. However, as a **gesture of goodwill** it is common to reward anyone who has been of assistance, whether they've driven you, carried your bags or simply performed a minor surgical procedure.

Most restaurant and hotel bills include a small **service charge** (10–15%) as well as a smaller charge (3–5%) for including the first charge. At the end of a meal, round your bill up to the next multiple of 10 (if the bill comes to ﹩73, give the waiter ﹩80). Porters who bring bags to your room should be given about ﹩30, or as much as it takes to get them to leave. Don't forget to tip the maids who clean your hotel room or there is a strong chance they will return and mess it up again. **Taxi drivers** should be tipped at least 10%, unless you're prepared to exit a moving vehicle. It is also not unusual for air passengers to tip their pilot following an incident-free landing.

In many country areas, people will be offended if you offer a tip – but accept it nonetheless – and, in fact, demand to be offended if you forget.

CASH MACHINES

Automatic teller machines are becoming more common throughout Molvania, although few ever contain money. Due to the country's erratic electrical supply it is often necessary to complete withdrawals with the aid of a mechanical **winch** handle located on the side of most machines.

> ### Traveller's Tip
> *Remember, when shopping in Molvania, be careful not to throw away your VAT receipts. There is no effective refund scheme but littering is an offence.*

FIREARMS

Strict laws governing firearms apply throughout Molvania and the list of those who may carry **hand-guns** is limited to police officers, soldiers, members of sporting shooters' associations, customs officials, parking officers, veterinary surgeons, postal workers, dental nurses, primary school teachers, anyone in regular employment and nuns.

SHOPPING

Molvanians love their traditional markets and street stalls; however, there are a few modern western-style **supermarkets** springing up. Despite appearances these establishments can be rather poorly-stocked and the service excruciatingly slow, especially the so-called Ezprezz 10 items or less check-out aisles, where it is not uncommon to see extended Molvanian families, each member clutching 10 items, painstakingly carrying up to 180 individual purchases.

VAT REFUND

Remember that upon leaving you are entitled to a **value-added tax** (VAT) refund on new goods valued at $ 5000 or more.

To claim your **refund**, look for the brown *Zcajajac* counter in the departure lounge of any Molvanian international airport. Show the official customs officer your purchase (and receipt!) and he will get you to fill in a refund form, which must then be stamped by another official at the opposite end of the terminal who will direct you to the nearest authorized VAT credit agency. Unfortunately, all refunds may only be given in local coins, the weight of which may, in turn, land you with an **excess baggage fee**.

> ### Traveller's Tip
> Many tourists visiting dining establishments worry about Molvania's reputation for over-charging foreign patrons. Our advice is not to worry. You most probably will be over-charged but don't be offended. This sort of low-level fraud is not meant personally; in fact, it's usually done with a smile. The truth is, many travellers arriving from Greece and Turkey are pleasantly surprised at how little they're over-charged.

There's no disputing the fact that Molvania is a shopper's paradise.

COMMUNICATIONS

TELEPHONE

The country code for calls to Molvania is 372. Lutenblag numbers with seven digits do not require an additional area code. Six-digit numbers require the area code 2. Eight-digit numbers beginning with 09 generally involve **pre-recorded messages** of a largely sexual nature.

Within Molvania most towns can be dialled directly, although in some cases you will require the assistance of an operator. Simply dial 01 and wait for a buzzing tone, which will generally be followed by the sound of someone clearing their throat loudly and cursing. This is the operator.

Most hotel rooms have telephones but using these can be quite expensive. A cheaper, if slightly less convenient, method of making calls is to visit a **public phone office** or *Cweveskid*. Make sure you are carrying plenty of coins and wait for a booth to become available. Then it's just a matter of placing a 10q coin in the slot before lifting the receiver and waiting for a dial tone at which point another 10q needs to be inserted. Dial your number and then as soon as it is answered put the remainder of your coins in.

Alternatively, you can purchase a *fornikarta* (phone-card) at any post office.

MOBILE PHONES

Mobile phone coverage outside the capital Lutenblag can be a little patchy and SMS text messaging – where available – still involves **Morse code**. However, Molvania operates one of the most extensive walkie-talkie networks in the world. These useful devices, many small enough to be carried in a modest day-pack, make communication possible in all but the most remote areas of the country.

INTERNET

Internet access has been slow in coming to Molvania and, at a top rate of just 17bps, many visitors still find that postcards actually arrive quicker than their emails. Despite this, numerous **e-cafes** have sprung up in most of the larger cities; however, these facilities attract a somewhat disreputable crowd of Web users who spend many hours logged onto Molvania's most visited Internet site www.nudigurlz.com.mv

---

In Case of Emergency...
The emergency telephone number throughout Molvania is ☎ 00990. Callers will be asked to give clear details of their situation and state whether they require police, ambulance or the arson investigation squad. Do not expect an immediate response as you will be speaking to a recorded message service; however, the tape is checked quite regularly.

LUTENBLAG
[Lutnblaag]

LUTENBLAG

Lutenblag was once viewed by other European capitals as something of a backward, provincial outpost, but if there was ever any truth to that, there certainly isn't today. Since playing host to a string of major international events, including the **1998 World Petanque Championships** and 2001's *Stverska!* Folklorique Dance Expo, Lutenblag has developed into a bustling, cosmopolitan city with a lively nightclub scene, a busy cultural calendar and a fairly reliable electricity supply to all but the outermost suburbs.

The city is not without its problems, pollution being one of the major drawbacks – many visitors have been struck by the thick blanket of smog that hangs over much of the town.

But things are looking up, with Molvania recently signing the **Kyoto Protocol** and announcing plans to phase out brown coal as an energy source. By 2010 all power generation will be diesel.

According to its motto, Lutenblag is the '**city of growth**', a claim that could be applied equally to its mushrooming suburbs as well as its current crime rate.

HISTORY

Lutenblag is situated in the centre of Molvania, on the banks of the **River Uze** and was originally made up of two towns, *Luten* ('place of many hills') and *Blag* ('municipal tip'), which joined in the 12th century. With the advent of more peaceful times, Lutenblag flourished as a city of merchants and craftsmen, becoming one of the great adult book printing centres of Europe. In fact, the world's first ever **pornographic lithograph** was published here in 1506. After a fire in 1654 much of the town was rebuilt in the baroque style. After another fire in 1951 it was rebuilt in concrete.

TOURIST INFORMATION

Your best source of information about Lutenblag is the **National Tourist Office** (*Offij Turizm Nazjonal*), which you will find at Av. Busjbusj (☎ 31769800). They're open Monday–Friday and, while very few of the staff speak English, they're very good at charades. In addition to stocking the standard range of **maps and brochures**, the office can arrange accommodation, car rental and, for a small additional fee, high-class adult escorts.

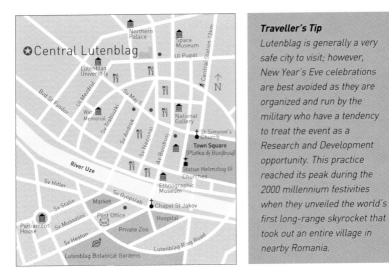

⦿Central Lutenblag

Northern Palace
Space Museum
Ul Pupat
Central Station 12km
Lutenblag University
Blvd St Fyodor
Ul Merdrok
Sv Frablupzk
Sv Maj 1
War Memorial
Sv Androk
Sv Naajnal
Av Busjbusj
National Gallery
St Simeon's Church
Town Square
(Platka dj Busjbusj)
River Uze
Statue Helmzlog III
Churches
Sv Hitler
Ethnographic Museum
Sv Gyopslab
Sv Stalin
Market
Chapel St Jakov
Sv Mussolini
Post Office
Hospital
Parliament House
Sv Heston
Private Zoo
Lutenblag Ring Road
Lutenblag Botanical Gardens
N

Traveller's Tip
Lutenblag is generally a very safe city to visit; however, New Year's Eve celebrations are best avoided as they are organized and run by the military who have a tendency to treat the event as a Research and Development opportunity. This practice reached its peak during the 2000 millennium festivities when they unveiled the world's first long-range skyrocket that took out an entire village in nearby Romania.

SUGGESTED ITINERARIES
Depending on the length of your stay, you might want to see and do the following things:

One day	Visit the Royal Palace (*Palatz Rojal*) and check out the Old City.
Two days	Take an extended tour of the Old City before exploring the many Roman ruins upstream along the River Uze.
Three days	One more really good look at the Old City and perhaps a picnic in the Botanical Gardens (*Jardn Botanjka*).
Four days	As above, plus a night out enjoying a show at the famous Concert Hall (*Konkerthausj*).
Five days	Good opportunity to get your washing done.
Six days	And write a few postcards.

SHOPPING
Many visitors to Molvania will want to take something home to remember their trip and Lutenblag certainly offers a wide range of options for the keen souvenir hunter. Of course, you want to be certain what you're purchasing is a genuine product and to this end the Molvanian government has established a network of shops selling **handicrafts** to tourists under the banner *Uzrec ej Molvania* ('Made in Molvania'). If you find any item bearing this sticker, you can be assured that it is both authentic and marked up by 62%.

HOW TO GET AROUND

Car A car is a good way of getting around, although like most cities, peak hour can get busy. Things weren't helped when the long-awaited **Lutenblag Ring Road** (*Kirklbaan*) was built directly through the centre of town. Most freeways have a transit lane open to motorcycles, taxis and livestock. Car-pooling is also popular, with incentives for more than 15 people on a tractor. Unleaded petrol is freely available; look for the word *Bleifrei* ('methylated spirits') at any outlet. Speed on Molvania's only **autobahn** is technically unlimited,

Life in the transit lane! This Molvanian worker heads off early for another day at the Stock Exchange.

although the numerous pot-holes and stretches of unsurfaced road make anything over 70kmh unlikely, if not hazardous. The **blood alcohol limit** is .12 (.15 on weekends), but drivers should not be unduly perturbed as results from the Traffic Police's Russian-made breath-testing units are inadmissible in a court of law.

Taxi Lutenblagian taxi drivers have unfortunately developed a reputation for dishonesty which, coupled with a lack of commitment in the personal hygiene department, has led to fewer people taking cabs around the city. Common sense is the key here – simply insist that the driver switches on his meter at the start of any trip and always be on the look-out for signs you may be taking the long way round, such as one reading 'German Border – 20kms'.

Train The rail system around Lutenblag is cheap and efficient, although visitors can find it a little on the complicated side. There are basically four types of train, although one no longer runs, which leaves three: **Express** (*Ezprezz*), **Fast** (*Rapijd*) and **Passenger** (*Commutken*). Reservations are compulsory on all Express trains and Fast Trains except Intercity Fast Trains for which you can purchase a ticket on board provided the trip is outbound and not taking place during a public holiday. Passenger trains have no reserved seating in first-class and no seating at all in third-class unless you count the roof. Most rail and bus companies will offer a discount to passengers with disabilities, however, a recent court ruling has declared that being drunk is no longer a recognized handicap. Senior citizen **discounts** (20%) also apply to all passengers over 90, however ID may be required.

Bicycle An English-language brochure entitled 'Seeing the City by Bike' is available from most bookstores as well as the casualty ward of the Lutenblag Public Hospital.

WHERE TO STAY

Lutenblag offers a wide range of accommodation options, the best of which are listed below. Prices are cheap by European standards and if you look around it's possible to find lodgings for under ҂100 per night. Of course, these will be pretty **basic** and travellers wanting a few more creature comforts should be looking to pay ҂200–260 per night; at this level you can expect all the usual features such as private bathrooms, TV, air-conditioning and spittoons.

$$$ Accommodation **Luxury**

At the top end you can't go past the **Rojal Palatz Hotjl** which, as its name suggests, is built directly opposite a particle board factory. 'The Palace' is generally regarded as one of the finest hotels in Molvania, combining modern service and facilities with olde worlde charm and plumbing. Rooms here are luxurious, to say the least, with full continental breakfast (i.e. a bread roll and orange lemonade) included in the tariff. Prices are understandably high, although you will save by booking a room during the winter off-season when the hotel is closed.

✉ *192 Sv Nazjonal*
☎ *19 1196*
🖷 *19 1197*
@ *palace@moldi.co.mv*
🍴 *56*
▤ *DC, MC, V*

The extensively refurbished Art Nouveau mansion **U Tri Hradjna** was recently voted 'Most Beautiful Hotel' by the readers of *Vision Euro* magazine, a quarterly publication catering for the visually impaired traveller. Though the rooms are a little on the small side, clever design features such as fold-down beds and a combined fax machine/trouser press mean there's still plenty of space to move.

✉ *233 Sv Nazjonal*
☎ *12 2531*
🖷 *12 2555*
@ *utri@molnet.co.mv*
🛏 *70*
▤ *DC, MC, V*

Note: The complimentary chocolates left on your pillow are purely decorative. If accidentally swallowed immediately contact the Lutenblag Poisons Hotline on ☎03-77633310.

Those seeking something a little more 'chic' might try the luxurious **Trybekka**, a newly-renovated boutique hotel that is modern, stylish and so minimalist that they've even done away with fire escapes. The 'Tryb' is one of the few gay-friendly hotels in Molvania and same-sex couples should have no trouble getting a room, provided it's not shared.

✉ *Av Busjbusj*
☎ *10 5836*
🖷 *10 5835*
@ *trybe@molnet.co.mv*
🛏 *40*
▤ *DC, MC, V*

$$ | Accommodation **Mid-Range**

Pensjon Zegmar is a cosy boarding house in a quiet residential haven close to the Museum, which makes a nice alternative to the big chain hotels. Some rooms afford stunning views out over the Old City; unfortunately these are reserved for staff only.

Note: The owners are reasonably friendly and speak English, but may charge for this.

✉ 22 Av Busjbusj
☎ 14 3805
🖷 14 3806
@ zegmar@mol.co.mv
🗝 16 🍴
🖃 DC, MC, V

The entrance to this stately, brick residence is all about muted style and comfort. In the lobby of **Jze Petra** a grand piano player greets guests with Molvanian show-tunes while discretely armed security guards move about keeping gypsy beggars at bay. The Petra is big on historical ambience (Emperor Vladzjic III's son Rzemec is said to have used the toilets here in 1856) and numerous antiques are on display including paintings, sculptures and the hotel's computer reservation system.

✉ 47 Sv Maj 1
☎ 19 6097
🖷 19 6098
@ jze@molnet.co.mv
🗝 12 🍴 ✎
🖃 DC, MC, V

Known for its 24-hour casino and popular discotheque, **Zizjkov** has long been popular with visiting rock stars and EU officials. The hotel has spacious, well-appointed rooms all with private bathroom and bar facilities.

Note: Two rooms are set aside for travellers with disabilities – though, strangely, these are in an attic reached only by several sets of stairs and a ladder.

✉ 52 Sv Maj 1
☎ 17 1884
🖷 17 1885
@ ziz@molnet.co.mv
🗝 12 🍴
🖃 V

Situated across from the railway station in a rather run-down section of Lutenblag, **Hotjl Oljanka** has developed a somewhat seedy reputation as a meeting place for criminals and shady characters. However, the oft-expressed fears about room security are much exaggerated and with the fitting of time-delay door locks, grille mesh windows and metal detectors in the lobby there hasn't been a kidnap or serious assault here since 1999.

✉ 72 Sv Androk
☎ 13 1636
🖷 13 1639
@ oljanka@moldi.co.mv
🗝 14 🍴 ✎
🖃 DC, MC, V

Another good mid-range accommodation option is the many **private rooms** available in Lutenblag. For as little as ⑤50 you can share a flat with an invalid pensioner or local resident serving a home detention sentence.

$ Accommodation **Budget**

Lutenblag is a backpackers' delight with numerous hostels and *pensiones* offering budget-priced rooms. The **Diagzop Hostjl** opposite the railway station is popular, despite the sometimes surly attitude of its heavily tattooed staff. Dorm beds in rather crowded rooms can be found here for as little as $25.

✉ *73 Sv Androk*
☎ *14 7791*
✆ *14 7792*
@ *diag@moldi.co.mv*
🛏 *162*

Note: There are no shower or bath facilities but you will find a discount car wash across the road.

Another equally cheap hostel is the **Majkvic Jverzte**, which is located in a peaceful neighbourhood, well away from traffic, noise and crowds. On the downside, it's a three-hour bus ride to the city outskirts – but at least the rooms are neat and regularly fumigated. Facilities are understandably basic with shared bathrooms and dormitory-style bunks. During the low-season there's also a 10% discount for students, although this status must be proved with an official ID card or some form of body-piercing.

✉ *14 Sv Jabba*
☎ *19 7828*
@ *majk@molnet.co.mv*
🛏 *56*
💳 *MC V*

Philippe writes...

"*After years of travel I've learnt a simple fact: you are never going to meet anyone truly interesting in a five-star hotel. To really experience a country you have to be cold, uncomfortable and woken at dawn by the sound of a local artisan clearing his throat and expectorating. You can keep your clean white sheets and air-conditioned lobbies – give me the unserviced cellar of a local pensione any time.*" P.M.

Guests staying at Hotjl Oljanka are picked up in the hotel's own courtesy truck.

HEALTH ALERT
BEDBUGS CAN OFTEN BE FOUND IN MOLVANIA'S CHEAPER HOTELS BUT ARE LESS LIKELY TO BE A PROBLEM AT HIGHER PRICED ESTABLISHMENTS WHERE CIGAR SMOKE NATURALLY FUMIGATES THE ROOMS.

WHERE TO EAT

Lutenblag's dining scene is vibrant and ever changing, with new establishments opening every month or so and older ones regularly being closed down by **sanitation** inspectors. Sadly, some restaurants, particularly the tourist-oriented ones, often fall into the habit of 'embellishing' tourists' bills. Authorities have cracked down on this practice but many unscrupulous operators still exist and it pays to closely check the various added 'cover charges' before paying. Typical entries include '**service provision**' (having a waiter), 'additional napery realignment' (folding your serviette), 'incendiary supplementation' (candles on the table) and, in one inner-city bistro, a **departure tax** of 12%.

Of course, the further you get out of town, the more limited your dining options, and often the only place to eat will be a *tavernja* (traditional tavern). In these establishments cutlery is often not available and food should be eaten with the right hand (never the left, which is reserved for washing and greeting members of the royal family).

We Were Wrong!
*The publishers wish to make it clear that Lutenblag's **Jhahmim Restaurant** features Lebanese food and dancing, and not – as our previous edition described – lesbian food and dancing. We apologise for the error. However, on a positive note, the proprietors of Jhahmim inform us they are booked out for the next three years.*

Folk musicians are often used by Molvanian restaurateurs as a means of encouraging diners to leave at the end of a meal.

$$$ Dining **Luxury**

The wrought-iron tables, vaulted ceilings and crisp white tablecloths of **Zvermej Kval** make this exclusive eatery the ideal place to enjoy a sophisticated meal. Why then the owners decided to turn the establishment into a karaoke bar remains a mystery, but it doesn't seem to have deterred the many eager patrons who flock here each night to eat, drink and drone.

✉ *131 Sv Nazjonal*
☎ *19 0245*
🖿 *DC, MC, V*
🎤

Romjaci is a cozy, elegant wine bar and restaurant that serves excellent food in a stylish setting. The menu has something for everyone – provided you like pork – and the service is good, if a little slow. Special touches include a popular outdoor garden (often closed due to wasps), a complimentary red rose for all female diners and a 5L carafe of house wine for the men.

✉ *5 Sv Nazjonal*
☎ *17 3865*
🖿 *DC, V*
🌿

Those seeking a slightly more lively dining experience should book a table at **Alic's Kabaret**, one of Lutenblag's most popular and entertaining dinner theatre restaurants. Flamboyant owner and chef Alic is something of a showman and inclined to get diners involved with his cooking by tossing eggs, twirling plates and spinning all manner of utensils past their ears. Don't even think about refusing to take part, because not only is Alic very persuasive, he has quite a temper.

✉ *140 Sv Nazjonal*
☎ *17 3199*
🖿 *DC, MC, V*

Note: Bookings are essential, as is protective clothing and headwear.

Foodies searching for the ultimate 'upmarket' place to eat in Lutenblag might care to visit the famous **Revolving Restaurant** (*Gastrodizzi*) where diners can sample fine food whilst enjoying a panoramic view of the city. Due to intermittent power supply the restaurant itself does tend to revolve rather slowly (a full rotation can take up to six months), but the stunning vistas from three floors up make the wait truly worthwhile.

✉ *140 Sv Maj 1*
☎ *12 4656*
@ *revolve@moldi.co.mv*

✌ *Traveller's Tip*
Many restaurants and hotels in Lutenblag are described as 'smoke-free', meaning that patrons are free to smoke throughout the premises.

$$ | Dining **Mid-Range**

Bright and spacious, **Kaça Napoljtana** is a buzzing pizzeria that serves up good meals along with salads and large carafes of house wine. It can get quite loud when full, as can the chef.

✉ *152 Sv Nazjonal*
☎ *14 7593*

The American-owned, Japanese food servery **The Sushi Train** has branches all over the world. Sadly, its Lutenblag operation was forced to shut a while back after a mechanical fault saw one diner lose several fingers reaching for a nori roll. Following an out-of-court settlement, The Sushi Train is now open for business again, but don't expect completely authentic Japanese food; most of it is deep fried, even the sashimi.

✉ *74 Sv Androk*
☎ *19 5738*

Despite its out-of-the-way location, **Nenja Olgja's** ('Aunty Olga's') is a perennial favourite among those looking for genuine country cooking. Built like an old style *tavernja*, Olgas resembles a typical Molvanian kitchen: chains of garlic dangle from the low wooden ceiling above tables set with stained red-and-white gingham cloths, while in the corner several chain-smoking old men will be getting violently drunk. The meals here are typically rustic: goose liver in paprika sauce, black pudding with cabbage and creamed lambs' brains, sausage-in-a-pot and, of course, entrail soup (a Molvanian standard from the days when Stalin tried to starve the population).

✉ *Ul Hoxha*
☎ *11 6499*

Note: Many cab drivers will refuse to pick up diners after a meal at Olgja's due to the high incidence of passengers vomiting inside the vehicle.

The Lutenblag Tavern offers traditional folk-dancing performances. Dinner & Show – ℥50. Dinner only – ℥75.

$ Dining **Budget**

Kisjipja is run by a married couple (if the arguments from within the kitchen are anything to go by) and specializes in light meals served at cafe-style tables. Keep an eye out for the specials board featuring interesting salads and the chef's 'Fish of the Month'. During summer, diners can eat outdoors at picnic-style tables in the large courtyard garden.

✉ 129 Av Busjbusj
☎ 15 4729
🍴

Note: Bring a can of insect repellent, which will not only keep the mosquitoes away, but can also be sprayed onto your food to improve the taste.

Yes, the ubiquitous American burger bar **McDonalds** has infiltrated Molvania, although, it should be said, not without a fight from local restaurateurs who fought long and hard against the arrival of this fast food establishment, fearful that its combination of high-fat, sugar-laden food served in a sterile, soulless environment would drive standards up.

✉ 75 Av Busjbusj
☎ 12 9038
▤ DC, MC, V

Bistroj Vjo Dzar is a 24-hour cafe not far from the railway station. The food is cheap, if a little bland, and the waiters can't be faulted as they're armed. Their thick soups are good value and the bottomless cups of coffee are a further drawcard, especially for members of Lutenblag's homeless community, several of whom took up the offer in 2001 and have been occupying the same table ever since.

✉ 78 Sv Androk
☎ 15 5328

Conveniently located not far from Lutenblag University, **Sadjevcis** cafe caters for the city's academics and intelligentsia and, as a consequence, is generally empty.

✉ 13 Sv Maj 1
☎ 19 3470

Lutenblag market remains one of the best places to pick up bargain-priced carp in all of Central Europe.

ENTERTAINMENT

CLASSICAL MUSIC

You should pay at least one visit to the **Lutenblag Concert Hall** (*konkerthausj*) to hear some music and enjoy the ambience of this unique building. In 1946 Molvania's most respected architect **Petjka Schovjen** was given the job of designing a venue that would embody the city's rich cultural heritage. His controversial tee-pee structure was finished in August 1948 and, while it successfully reflected his passion for the American Indian culture, it failed to reflect certain principles of tensile strength in metals, and collapsed two months later during a mild storm. It was extensively re-modelled in the 1950s and is now home to the **Lutenblag Symphony Orchestra**, who give regular recitals. Works from the **National Opera of Molvania** are also performed here, but less frequently due to their complexity, length and lack of recognisable melodic form. Most works also require the use of up to a dozen Molvanian *bashken* horns that, whilst extraordinary in mountain valleys, are considered a hearing hazard in closed spaces.

FOLK & TRADITIONAL PERFORMANCE

Many venues cater for folk music and the **Kzamailkia Cultural House** (*Jignstumpf*) also presents traditional Molvanian puppet shows each evening at 7pm. These highly-stylised wooden marionettes are used to re-enact simple morality tales – except on Saturdays when an 11pm late show features an **adults-only** performance.

PUBS & CLUBS

There are many clubs and discotheques in Lutenblag where you can party all night long – however, chances are you'll be on your own as most locals prefer an early night. Jazz lovers should head downtown to **Bje Bjop**, a funky basement club; admission is free, although there is a small cover charge to help with the fire insurance premiums. Lutenblag even has its own Irish-themed pub **Vlad O'Reilljys** where the home-sick traveller can relax with a traditional pint of Guinness and a plate of pickled beetroot before getting into a fist-fight with a belligerent fellow drinker.

Nightlife - Lutenblag style!

HIGHLIGHTS

Any tour of the city must include a stop at the **Royal Palace** (*Palatz Rojal*), a famous landmark and home to Molvania's much-loved Royal Family in exile. Outside the main gates heavily armed guards stand on sentry duty. These flamboyantly dressed militiamen in their **distinctive grey pants** and highly plumed helmets are members of the King's own troops, the **Bazurkas**, who have been protecting the Palace since the Night of a Thousand Spoons in 1754 (see 'History' section). Each morning they parade past the Palace entrance in a loosely choreographed formation that has been described as not so much a march as a melee. Feel free to stop and take photos, although don't be surprised if one of them takes a shot at you.

Without doubt the best way to get a taste of Lutenblag's historical past is to take a walking tour of the **Old City**. Enter through a narrow gate on the northern side and on your left you will see an ancient **Roman column** that was originally used as a pillory but now serves as a mobile phone transmission tower for Molvania-Telski.

Reach for the Stars...

No visit to Lutenblag would be complete without a stop at the **Molvanian Space Museum**, where visitors can learn of the country's major role in the early Russian space program. During the late 1950s Molvanian scientists designed and built the first spacecraft to be fuelled by refined mineral turpentine. Tragically, *Splutfab I* exploded on launch, killing its entire crew and stripping paint from buildings within a 5km radius. *Splutfab II* was more successful and, in 1963, Molvania became the first nation to successfully land a man on Poland.

Madame Tussaud's has recently opened a museum in Lutenblag, featuring the world's largest collection of bearded men.

All the World's a Stage!

Just off Lutenblag's main square you'll find the historic **Workers' Theatre**, a small venue built during the Soviet Era, where anti-government plays about social justice and political reform were frequently performed. The acoustics at this theatre were said to be so good that one could whisper on stage and be clearly heard in the Information Ministry building across the road.

Behind this column is the town square and in the north-east corner of the square you will see **St Simeon's Church** (Crkja Simun), which was extensively damaged during World War II. Since then there have been ongoing restoration works and some of the scaffolding used actually dates back to 1948. The church, commemorating the **patron saint of poverty**, is open to the public (admission 𝔖120) and inside you will find some magnificent works of 14th century craftsmanship. The **sarcophagus** of St Simeon stands 2.3m-high, its front depicting scenes from the holy man's life, including his birth, early years as a preacher and unconventional ascent into heaven on the back of a scantily-clad virgin.

On the opposite side of the main square is an excellent **ethnographic museum** (*muzm ethnojgrafkskro*) featuring a large collection of Molvanian cutlery. Admission is free, although there is a 𝔖90 fee for passing through the front door.

At the northern end of the city are the remains of Lutenblag's **Old Fort**, an impressive stone structure that over the years has withstood attacks from Turks, Huns, Mongols and Tartars. Sadly, it was a Slovakian property developer who finally succeeded in demolishing the magnificent battlements in order to make room for an apartment block.

The famous **statue of Helmzlog III** (the 'Liberator of Lutenblag') stands in the centre of the busy main square, holding aloft a sword and what was for years assumed to be a shield, but has recently turned out – upon closer examination – to be the grille from a Fiat 350.

Just outside the Old City in a pleasant neighbourhood called Zamocja you will find a red brick house at 20 Av. Verbek. There is a small **plaque** outside recording the fact that it was in this house during World War II that local merchant **Jorg Grekjez** sheltered 45 Lutenblag Jews during the Nazi occupation. As their number grew, two large cellars were dug to conceal them and these brave people survived for several years living in cramped, foetid, airless conditions. These days the cellars are used for student accommodation.

> **Traveller's Tale**
> As well as many fine exhibits, the **Lutenblag Museum of Local History** offers a video presentation entitled 'Treasures from the Past'. One reader wrote to inform us that the presentation was unsuitable for children due to its length, volume and frequent graphic depictions of medieval torture. There were also racist overtones in its presentation of Molvanian gypsies.

Regarded by many as one of the finest examples of Renaissance architecture in Europe, the beautiful **Chapel of St Jakov** was built between 1431 and 1536. Initially it was only supposed to be a simple church with one nave, but the town leaders expressed a wish for a more impressive building and over the course of construction various features were added, including transepts, apses and an underground **billiard room**. The chapel is officially closed to the public, but for a small 'tip' the man at the door will grant you access. For an extra tip he'll even say mass for you.

For a slightly more 'modern' experience, a visit to the **Lutenblag Stock Exchange** (143 Zvordem Placa) is well worth the trip. Here you can see Molvania's corporate high-flyers, most of whom have made their fortune in concrete, wheel and deal. Official trading begins at 9.30am when the President of the Stock Exchange fires an AK-47 into the air. Tours Mon-Fri 9.30am.

> **Philippe writes...**
> "Art lovers have much to look forward to in Lutenblag with the Galljeri Nazjonal ('National Gallery') drawing thousands of visitors each year. They have a pretty impressive international collection here, including works from Rembrandt, Van Gogh, Titian and Picasso, stolen from all over Europe during World War II. But for those prepared to look beyond the obvious glitz of such populularist offerings I'd have to recommend a little gallery at 413 Sv. Medezeni called The Vcetrezen. The style here is minimalist, but the work on display absolutely stunning. One room was entirely empty except for a small fire-hose attached to the wall. Lesser students of art than I would no doubt have walked past this tightly-coiled installation, oblivious to the joyful irony of its juxtaposition. Bravissimo! " *P.M.*

A short distance south of the Museum is a well-kept park in which a small **private zoo** has been established. The zoo houses a large selection of wild cats, birds and mammals, unfortunately all in the one cage, and is open Mon–Sat. during the summer months. Clearly, stocks may vary. In past years many visitors would come here to see the extremely rare *bvoric*, a **single horned goat** native to Molvania but, sadly, this specimen passed away in 1993. However, thanks to advances in the twin fields of taxidermy and animatronics, a passable replica is still on display.

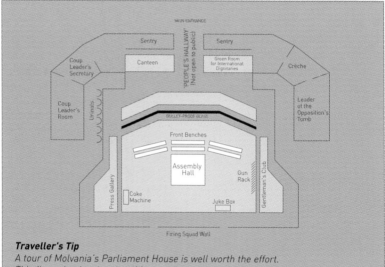

Traveller's Tip
A tour of Molvania's Parliament House is well worth the effort.
This floor plan is a handy guide.

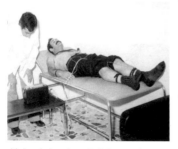

Molvania has long led the way in scientific achievements. In 1959 Prof. V. C. Ulcviecel pioneered the world's first ever electrolysis machine, seen here testing it out on his mother.

The **Museum of Science and Technology** (*Muszm Skjenteknolojyka*) celebrates Molvania's many scientific achievements, including the invention of callipers, blue carnations and the harpoon. There is also a special exhibit dedicated to **Jzeovak Tkermec** (1936–1994), one of Molvania's most brilliant scientists. Tkermec was a pioneer in the field of genetic engineering and, in 1987, he succeeded in grafting a human ear onto a mouse. But his greatest breakthrough came a year later when he successfully managed to graft a mouse onto a human ear.

For those seeking relief from the hustle and bustle of this busy city, take a stroll through the beautifully landscaped **Lutenblag Botanical Gardens**. Here you can stop and admire numerous specimens of the Molvanian rose (right), a locally bred variety that produces no flowers or leaves, just thorns. In summer you can rent boats from the kiosk, which is good fun, although ultimately pointless as there is no water for 200km. Entrance fee to the gardens is $120 and you will be handed three coloured tickets: one for general admission, one for the herbarium and another that entitles you to enjoy the **lawned areas** as well as vote in municipal elections. Make sure you hang onto each one, as the park inspectors (*Polizi Parzca*) are not only active, but heavily armed.

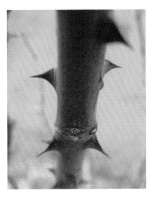

Finally, no visit to Lutenblag would be complete without a viewing of its famous **War Memorial** (*Miljtakslaab*). This massive marble monument, near the centre of the Old City, is dedicated to the estimated 18,000 Molvanian soldiers who fought abroad during World War II and never returned. Some were killed, the majority deserted and many are believed to be still living in Western Europe as illegal immigrants.

Spend a Penny...
Visitors to Lutenblag's main square are often puzzled by a small, wrought-iron structure opposite the Town Hall. Built as part of the 1896 international trade fair, this prototype is one of the world's first and only female urinals. It still operates, although first-time users are advised to bring a change of shoes.

The historic Royal Lutenblag Tennis Club was extensively damaged during the civil war but has now been re-opened. Players are reminded of the need to hose and bag the court as well as check for unexploded mines.

Sjerezo

Lake Debrizca

Vajana

River Ierko

River Fiztula

The Great Plain

Gyrorik

River Fiztula

MOLVANÎAN ALPS

Lake Bzejenko

Svetranj

River Vzintga

Posterwaji Ranges

THE MOLVANÎAN ALPS
[Alpj Molvanjka]

THE REGION

Picture a cosy alpine cottage covered in snow, its frosted windows glowing with the light of a large log fire as it warms the chilled night air. Welcome to summer in the Molvanian Alps. This unique mountain region towering above the mighty **River Fiztula** has for years been overlooked as a holiday destination. But now, thanks to **improved tourist facilities**, coupled with a cease-fire in the war with Romania, visitors are beginning to discover the charm of this forgotten jewel.

Running from the fertile plains of the River Jerko basin all the way east to the mighty Postenwalj Mountains, the Molvanian Alps region offers a wide range of travel options. Naturally, there is wonderful skiing with over 2000km of groomed and fully mine-swept trails to suit all skill levels. Nature-buffs, too, will be delighted with the area's numerous national parks, havens to many of Molvania's rare and endangered species of flora and fauna. Here you can trek the famous **Valentinji Promendjj** ('Lover's Walk') amidst the beauty of forested slopes covered in cyclamen, heather, gorse and used **prophylactics**.

Svetranj is the region's major city and administrative centre. A bustling, exciting town set on the banks of the River Jerko, it provides the ideal stepping-off point for a tour of this fascinating area. Then there's the awesome grandeur of the **Great Plain** (*Planja Grandj*), recently granted UNESCO World Heritage status as a 'site of significant monotony'. Finally, don't forget to include at least one trip north to Vajana, home to Molvania's famous free-range zoo; if possible make your visit on the first Sunday of each month so you can watch the animals being fed.

The Great Plains, recently granted UNESCO World Heritage status as a 'site of significant monotony'.

Philippe writes...

" *I first visited the south of Molvania nearly 20 years ago before anyone else had discovered its charms. Back then there were no restaurants, no hotels and not even potable water. It was a truly authentic travel experience. Now you'll see well-heeled tourists relaxing in soulless, westernized bars and restaurants, oblivious to the fact that I was there first.* "   P.M.

SVETRANJ

As recently as the 1960s, Svetranj was considered the playground of Molvania's rich and famous who were drawn to the region by its bracing climate, **stunning scenery** and relaxed attitudes to underage sex. These days Svetranj still retains many of the same charms that made the town such a popular destination. One of its major attractions would, without doubt, have to be the old city **castle**, believed by many to be the setting for the Molvanian version of *Romeo and Juliet*, called *Slobadril un Mustaza*, written by a local author in the **16th century**. Every day tourists can be seen here testing out their thespian skills on the castle's balcony as they utter those immortal lines *'Slobadril, Slobadril, uch ver az tje?'*. Like the star-crossed lovers of this **literary classic**, you too will fall in love with Svetranj.

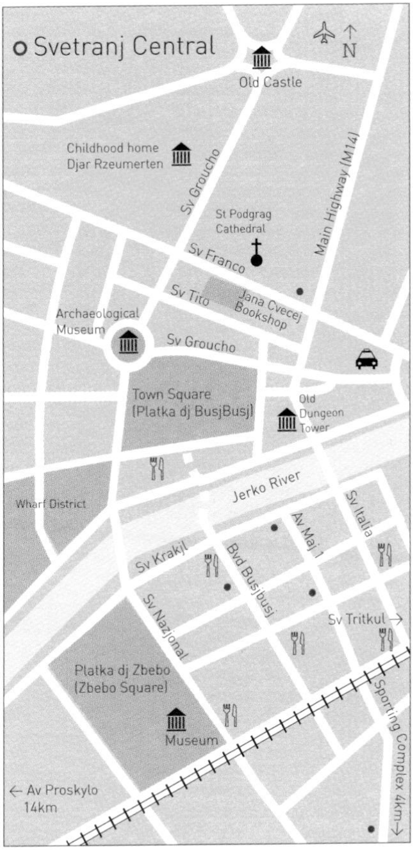

o Svetranj Central

Old Castle

Childhood home
Djar Rzeumerten

Sv Groucho

St Podgrag
Cathedral

Main Highway (M14)

Sv Franco

Sv Tito

Jana Cvecej
Bookshop

Archaeological
Museum

Sv Groucho

Town Square
[Platka dj BusjBusj]

Old
Dungeon
Tower

Jerko River

Wharf District

Sv Krakjl

Bvd Busjbusj

Av Maj.1

Sv Italia

Sv Nazjnal

Sv Tritkul →

Platka dj Zbebo
[Zbebo Square]

Museum

Sporting Complex 4km →

← Av Proskylo
14km

HISTORY

One of the most important **commercial centres** in southern Molvania, the city of Svetranj was established in the 16th century as a trading post. Being a frontier town, a series of heavily-fortified **battlements** were built soon after to guard against possible Turkish attack from the south. Unfortunately, the Turks attacked from the east and the village was razed before extensive re-building during the 18th century saw it emerge as a major regional centre. Today the city is famous for its handicrafts, especially the locally-produced **Svetranj lace**, which has been compared favourably with Brussels and Venetian Reticella lace, despite being a little coarser and made from hessian. Other local produce includes leather-goods and low-grade heroin.

ORIENTATION

As you leave the central railway station turn left and make your way up the **Platka dj Zbebo** towards the town hall. Here you will find some excellent shops and welcoming outdoor cafes. On the right, just before the town hall gates, is one of the oldest and most beautiful **chateaux** in Svetranj. The fact the building is now a **pinball parlour** in no way detracts from its architectural significance and a visit is well worthwhile. Numerous interesting lanes and alleyways lead off from the Platka, or city square, and all provide a good opportunity to explore the town centre, although visitors are advised against wandering into the neighbourhoods bordering the River Jerko after dark or during the day.

The riverfront itself is a delightful mix of terrace cafes and outdoor eateries. Sadly, the regular number of large delivery trucks parked outside often obscures the otherwise **delightful vista**. This, in addition to the fumes from their idling diesel motors, can serve to diminish the open-air dining experience, but it remains a must for those seeking the genuine Svetranj ambience. After a quick coffee here you're well placed to explore the hustle and bustle of the riverside **market stalls** featuring butchers, bakers and other assorted traders. This timeless setting is a marvellous place to simply wander and soak in the atmosphere: the sights, the smells and, of course, the sounds as the stall-holders utter their traditional cry *'Haltz! Jzorban!'* ('Stop! Thief!').

SHOPPING

Svetranj remains one of the best places in Europe to obtain **discount merchandise** and despite threats of legal action you can still pick up a pair of genuine Nikey or Reeboq runners for a fraction of the usual cost. DVDs are also cheap and plentiful, although visitors are reminded that Molvania is officially classified as **Region 7** (meaning its recordings can only be played on equipment manufactured in Molvania or northern Bulgaria). Visitors are also advised against purchasing electrical equipment unless you're going camping and may have need to start a fire.

Svetranj produces one of the few televisions in the world to come with its own built-in sprinkler system.

HOW TO GET THERE

Nestled on the banks of the River Jerko, Svetranj can be reached by either road or rail. The main highway south from Lutenblag is known as the M14 and was originally a **toll road**. Fees have long ago been abolished; however, some visitors have recently reported being stopped by locals posing as toll collectors and demanding cash, cigarettes or a lift.

There is also a small airport on the city's northern outskirts, but it was closed by **civil aviation authorities** in 1998 after a Swiss passenger jet on final approach narrowly avoided colliding with a mule tethered to a wind-sock.

Train Traveller's Tip
Svetranj's grandly built Central Station is in fact some 12km from the city centre.

The Age of Discovery

Svetranj is noted for being the birthplace of Molvania's most famous explorer, the legendary **Jolp Trubazbor.** On 13 June, 1468, Trubazbor and his brave crew left Lutenblag with three sailing ships. It took them nearly a month to carry them over the mountains, but eventually they reached the Baltic Sea where they set off in search of the elusive East Indies. Inexplicably, they travelled north-west, ending up in Scandinavia where  Trubazbor put up a Molvanian flag and declared that southern Sweden would henceforth be called '**Jolpland**'. Under a hail of arrows he and his crew retreated, sailing back across the Baltic Sea. Weeks of raping, pillaging and plundering then ensued until Trubazbor was eventually forced to close the ship's Games Room. By this stage he'd reached Poland where things went from bad to worse. It was here, on a bitterly cold and moonless night, near the port of **Gdansk**, that he lost two of his ships in a card game. Refusing to accept defeat, the expedition continued and in 1471 Trubazbor (armed with spices, slaves and treasure) eventually made it back home where he was given a traditional hero's welcome – he was robbed.

WHERE TO STAY

Finding suitable accommodation in Svetranj can be somewhat confusing because the city has adopted its own system of star ratings, ranging from six (luxury international hotels) through to one (refugee detention centres). When it comes to cost, obviously location is the key; the further your hotel is from the centre of Svetranj, the more you can expect to pay. When booking, keep in mind that if you want a room with a double bed, it should be specifically requested; otherwise, you are likely to get a room with twin beds or – for a large additional cost – a room with twins in a bed.

$$$ Accommodation Luxury

Although a little out of town, one of the most historic lodging houses in Svetranj is the impressive **Ozjbrej Kastl**. The first recorded mention of this medieval mansion is from a 1252 register of municipal interests. The most recent mention is from a 2002 Department of Sanitation advisory report into the hotel's restaurant. The 'Ozj' offers luxurious rooms and opulent decor that is almost Viennese in style, although the service and facilities are pure Molvanian.

✉ 90 Av Maj 1
☎ 51 5698
🖷 51 5697
@ ozji@molnet.co.mv
🛏 58 ᵀᴵᵀ ✎
▤ DC, MC, V

For the more active visitor who doesn't mind being a few kilometres out of town, **Hotjl Zport** is an excellent option. Located adjacent to the Svetranj Sporting Complex, it boasts a running track, squash courts and an Olympic-sized settling pond. The hotel even has its own soccer pitch and each Saturday organizes a staff-versus-visitor match.

✉ 267 Av Maj 1
☎ 50 0696
🖷 50 0697
@ sport@moldi.co.mv
🛏 200 ᵀᴵᵀ
▤ DC, MC, V

Note: Guests are strongly advised to avoid taking part in these contests due to reports of frequent and escalating on-field violence, particularly on the part of the concierge.

Gzizco Hzorbec is one of Svetranj's oldest hotels. It is built on a hill overlooking the city; however due to some architectural oversight, all the rooms face back into the hill. On the positive side, guests will not be disturbed by an excess of natural light or air.

✉ Sv Franco
☎ 55 3856
🖷 55 3855
@ gzizco@molnet.co.mv
🛏 54 ᵀᴵᵀ

$$ Accommodation **Mid-Range**

Close to the river, the **Hotjl Jerko** overlooks the bustling wharf district and is a mere stone's throw from the city square (a fact confirmed during the civil riots of 1997 when several windows were shattered by unruly protestors). The hotel offers a relaxed, informal service although one guest did report being physically threatened after arriving several minutes late for breakfast.

✉ *75 Sv Krakjl*
☎ *56 2314*
🖷 *56 2315*
@ *jerko@moldi.co.mv*
🛏 *29*　🍴
🖻 *DC, MC*

The **Zibberief Hotjl** is a small, family-run establishment that is centrally located and comfortable with clean, modern rooms to suit most budgets. The hotel, like its owner's teeth, has undergone extensive renovation work and most rooms offer TV and private bathrooms.

✉ *33 Bvd Busjbusj*
☎ *59 5696*
🖷 *59 5697*
@ *zibber@moldi.co.mv*
🛏 *18*　🍴
🖻 *DC, MC, V*

$ Accommodation **Budget**

The owners of the 15th century *pensione* **Plepjic Vaz** describe it as 'conveniently placed', which may be true for them – they live next door – but for guests the hotel is some 14km west of the city. The slightly drab decor of the rooms is brightened up by the presence of pot plants and a variety of colourful bathroom mould.

✉ *354 Av Proskylo*
☎ *52 5600*
🛏 *24*
🖻 *V*

Svetranj also offers a wide range of youth hostel accommodation, a cheap alternative to hotels. Bookings are essential as these places can get pretty busy in summer, especially now that the largest and most popular hostel, **Djormi's**, has been closed down by authorities after guests reported finding video cameras hidden in the women's shower facilities. (The owner, the irrepressible Viktor Djormi, originally denied all knowledge, then insisted the cameras were there for security to prevent soap and towel theft. The matter is still before the courts where a full bench of judges are now into their second year of viewing the taped evidence).

Closed pending criminal investigations

WHERE TO EAT

As the culinary capital of the Molvanian Alps district, Svetranj prides itself on fine dining. The signature dish in upmarket restaurants here is *pvork zpiitka* (**roast pig** served with an apple in its mouth). This is a difficult meal to prepare as the traditional recipe calls for the apple to be inserted whilst the pig is still alive. Meanwhile, visitors seeking a slightly more **casual dining experience**, and who are prepared to brave the cigarette smoke and deep-fried food, might care to drop by a *vzarjkil* (health food bar).

$$$ Dining Luxury

Without doubt, Svetranj's most popular restaurant is **Kisbzucten**, located right on the city's main square. Meals here are filling, with typical dishes generally involving cabbage, cream, potatoes, sausages and offal. And that's entree. The less ravenous diner might try ordering something lighter like a bowl of *guzpa* (a thick soup made from paprika and goose lard).

✉ 23 Platka dj Busjbusj
☎ 55 5330
▭ DC, MC, V

A 20-minute drive east of the city will take you to **Kbadi**, a large, authentic *tavernja* specializing in rustic cuisine. It's also a very popular establishment and being so far out of town it can be difficult getting a cab home on busy nights. One option is to take a cab there and then invite your driver in for a light meal. Most are happy to do so in return for a bowl of soup and 2L carafe of house wine.

✉ 243 Sv Tritkul
☎ 52 1246
▭ MC, V

Note: This is a good way of ensuring you'll have transport home, the only downside being that you may have to do the driving.

Book early for a seat at any one of Svetranj's popular street cafes (tables cost extra).

$$ Dining **Mid-Range**

Another culinary institution in the centre of town is **Zad Gjorjze** (George's Pad), a large eatery that serves hearty regional dishes, many baked in a traditional *petzda* (petrol-burning oven). Come early to enjoy jazz and all-in brawling.

✉ *54 Bvd Busjbusj*
☎ *54 7834*

For the ultimate outdoor dining experience make a booking at **Tjuj Meda**, a provincial-style eatery directly opposite the Museum. During summer you can sit under the massive oak tree drinking local beer and soaking in the atmosphere. Bookings are essential on Saturday nights when large crowds often gather for a traditional Svetranj feast in which a wild pig is killed by hand and roasted on a spit (though not necessarily in that order) before being devoured by hungry patrons.

✉ *12 Sv Nazjonal*
☎ *59 7830*
🍴

$ Dining **Budget**

Visitors in search of a light snack should cross the river and visit **Bistroj Cravben**, a friendly little cafe not far out of town. It's run by a local couple and the menu is changed frequently. Unfortunately, the same cannot be said for the table linen.

✉ *54 Sv Italia*
☎ *50 2655*

Kaça Zrzaveho (literally 'Stink House') is a surprisingly popular restaurant close to the centre of the city. Each dish here appears lovingly prepared with the freshest ingredients. This is, of course, an illusion as most of the meals are pre-packaged and snap-frozen in a Slovakian processing plant.

✉ *76 Bvd Busjbusj*
☎ *51 2765*

Fishy Business #2!

Located on the River Jerko, the restaurants of Svetranj naturally pride themselves on the wide range of fine fish available. Trout, pike, cod and a rare form of fresh-water dolphin are all regularly featured on local menus – but without doubt the most sought-after delicacy is the exotic *kjerzenko* fish. Unique to the region, this gastronomical treat is actually highly toxic and must be prepared and served only by qualified chefs. As part of the process a small, oily gland just behind the fish's head is carefully removed. This gland – the only edible part of the fish – is then cooked while the rest of the body is thrown away or used as a poultry feed supplement.

HIGHLIGHTS

A good way to explore the city is via the River Jerko and **small boats** (*plunkas*) are available for hire at the **Svetranj boatsheds**. These colourfully decorated craft cost just $20 per hour (although oars will set you back an extra $100) and a leisurely voyage downstream will take you past many architectural delights, including the **old dungeon tower** (*kzmurta*) where suspected felons were routinely interrogated with hot pokers before being cast from the roof to a **grisly death** on the rocks below. Fortunately, this form of summary justice was abolished in 1978, but the tower remains a potent reminder of Molvania's savage past.

The picturesque Jerko River.

The **Svetranj Cathedral** sits high on a flood-plain overlooking the city. Two building phases are clearly discernible: the lower part is indebted to the late-Gothic style, while the cupola and dome owe much to 20th century advances in aluminium cladding.

The **Svetranj Archaeological Museum** is open every day except Monday, Wednesday, Thursday and weekends and contains an impressive collection of artefacts: Liburnian bronze jewellery, numerous **Roman relics** and a lock of pubic hair claimed to be from a 13th century Catholic bishop. Tours of the Museum are offered and most visitors reported the guides to be very informative and helpful, although a little threatening towards anyone attempting to leave early.

Bu-Bu the Reformer

Out the front of the Unjverstat Politikat you will see a **statue** of former Prime Minister 'Bu-Bu' holding up three fingers (the only ones he had left after a 1932 cutlery accident). This pose commemorates his achievement in legislating to ensure separation of powers between the three arms of Molvanian federal authority: the judiciary, the legislature and the mafia.

One of the finest features of Svetranj is its long **central boulevard**, shaded by a double line of plane trees. Cafes and restaurants line this strip and each evening during the **summer months** locals turn out here in their finest clothes for the twilight *passegjeco* (promenade), a chance for Svetranj high society to see and be seen. Sadly, the pleasure of this ritual has been somewhat diminished in recent years by the way it often coincides with a sharp rise in **home burglaries**, thought to be the work of gypsy opportunists.

Down a small lane diagonally opposite the Cathedral you'll find the **Jana Cvecej Bookshop**, one of Svetranj's most famous stores. It was set up in 1957 by Jana Cvecej, a keen book collector and prolific author in her own right, who was worried by the lack of decent literature available in the city. The shop now boasts over 7000 titles, the only drawback being that they're all books written by Cvecej herself.

A Deep Thinker...
Just to the north of Svetranj at 1120 Sv. Livisnki Obala you will find a humble-looking stone residence that was actually the birthplace and **childhood home of Djar Rzeumerten**, arguably Molvania's most famous philosopher. Born in 1768, Rzeumerten was an advanced thinker whose greatest achievement was to actually prove that he did not exist.

Djar Rzeumerten

Svetranj locals gather each year on 6 June to celebrate the Feast of the Lop-Sided Saints.

THE GREAT PLAIN

In stark contrast to the mighty alps towering just a few hundred kilometres to the east, the flat expanse surrounding Svetranj was once known to the Romans as *Plana Monotona Desolata*. The vegetation here is typical of central Molvania – thistles and weeds interspersed by barren, rocky patches. The **expansive beauty** of this exposed land seems to stretch on forever, and over the centuries it has attracted painters, poets, romantics and cement-mining consortiums. But, of course, since time immemorial this **massive prairie** has been home to *cziksos* (shepherds) who, even today, can be seen moving their flocks across the bleak, **windswept landscape**. These colourful figures still wear traditional costume, although their horses have, in most cases, been replaced by noisy, three-wheeled motorbikes imported from Ukraine. (The bikes are, however, still steered using reigns). Accompanying each *czikso* is a large herd of sheep and several *zuti* herd dogs. Interestingly, the sheep are kept for their wool and milk, while the dogs are **routinely slaughtered** for their meat, considered a delicacy by these nomadic shepherd-folk.

WHEN TO GO

One of the best times to visit the Great Plain is September, when the annual **wine harvest** gets under-way. Being a deeply religious community the entire event is punctuated by masses and special ceremonies, the highlight of which takes place on 22 September when the first grapes are crushed by a young virgin girl (often brought in from Hungary due to a lack of suitably qualified locals). Mid-winter also has its charm as this is the time that the region's highly sought-after **truffle crop** is harvested. Visitors can watch as **specially trained pigs** scour the plains sniffing out the elusive delicacy that, once located, is then dug up using traditional methods such as explosives or a small front-end loader.

Let the festival begin!
There are dozens of small villages, many containing just a few hundred people, dotted across the Great Plain. Most of these delightful communities have regular festivals that are usually filled with drinking, dancing and fighting. These are known as *vecborjas* (weekends) and tourists are generally welcome.

Cattle on the Great Plain have been genetically-modified to grow just two legs. Whilst this feature reduces meat yield, it does make the muster considerably easier.

Philippe writes...

"*I was travelling through Svetranj some years ago with a group of friends who suddenly had to leave me. Tired of the usual tourist traps and tacky souvenir shops, I hailed a cab and asked the driver (in my best Molvanian!) to take me somewhere I could get a real sense of the country's heart and soul, somewhere I belonged. Two and a half hours up the road he dropped me off in a vast wilderness that I later recognized as the Great Plain. A few days later when I collapsed from hunger and hypothermia I realized it was one of the most authentic travel experiences I'd ever had. Unforgettable!*"

P.M.

HOW TO GET AROUND

The best way to sample this unique rural landscape is as part of a guided 4WD tour. Several operate, the most common being Zvedir Zafarji, which offers two-, five- and seven-day **adventure packages**. They follow ancient herding trails across the plain, with accommodation in traditional **animal-skin tents**. It doesn't take long for you to realize just how tough, cold, bleak and monotonous life out here must have been and Zvedir Zafarji tours certainly capture all the elements of this experience.

WHERE TO STAY

The less adventurous might consider spending a night or two at **The Great Plain Ranch**, situated about 25km east of Svetranj. Guests can spend the night in authentic dung-covered *stinkas* (traditional huts) and be entertained by local cowboys performing their highly popular **equestrian show**. These talented riders display enormous control over their horses, making them stop, turn, leap and twist with the slightest touch from an **electronic prod**. Shows run every weekend throughout the year, although in bad weather they're staged in the ranch's Mess Hall, which can get a little crowded. Bookings essential.

The Great Plain area has also seen a rise in *aggro-turizm*, with several properties offering overnight accommodation and excellent home-cooking combined with the opportunity to experience life on a **working farm**. Sadly, this program has been temporarily suspended, but the local tourism bureau hopes to have it running again as soon as the region is officially declared anthrax-free.

VAJANA

Until recently this medieval town was a warren of slums, clustering round a polluted lake near the festering rubbish-strewn foothills of **Mount Toxyk**. It was hardly the sort of place to attract holiday-makers, although the city did pick up a municipal 'Tidy Town' award in 1976. This accolade prompted something of a revival for Vajana and these days it is considered a first-rate tourist destination offering **modern comforts** and an exciting nightlife – despite a 10pm militarily enforced curfew. Visitors looking to combine a bit of adult entertainment with local culture should pay a visit to **Spredzelegz**, one of the few Folkloric Lap Dancing venues in Europe.

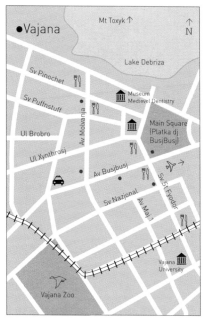

HISTORY

This ancient city was founded back in AD 720 by the great matriarch, **Besbolja**. She was referred to as 'Mother of All Vajanans', probably because the population at the time was 14 and they were all her children. In the 15th century, Vajana was called Molvania's 'cultural melting pot' as it had a large melting pot into which ethnic minorities were lowered during the **Balkan Inquisition**.

During the Middle Ages Vajana doctors pioneered complex medical procedures. This lithograph shows physicians amputating a limb whilst simultaneously extracting a confession.

HOW TO GET THERE

Road The main road from Svetranj across the plains into Vajana is single lane for much of its length, heavily pot-holed and often closed due to snow, rock falls or chemical spills. Before embarking on any trip along this treacherous stretch of highway, drivers are strongly advised to contact the **Vajana Police Headquarters** (☎06/43677214) and leave details of when you are planning to set off, when you expect to arrive and – in the event of trouble – whether you'd like your remains buried or cremated.

Trucks carrying illegal immigrants pause to enjoy a scenic stop on the Svetranj – Vajana highway.

Air Air travel into Vajana is a good option for those wishing to avoid a long road trip. Commuter flights land regularly at **Ruzbcil Airport**, named after one of Molvania's most distinguished aviation scientists, Hlavni Ruzbcil (1952–1997), the man who first proved a link between smoking during aircraft re-fuelling and fiery death. Sadly, he passed away in the process.

HOW TO GET AROUND

Vajana is a relatively small city, divided into quarters of which there are three. Unfortunately, **public transport** is slow and unreliable so taxis are generally your best bet. There is a glut of car hire firms in Vajana, which has pushed prices down, but visitors should be wary of excessively discounted vehicles as they may lack modern features such as power steering or brakes.

Old Vajana.

New Vajana.

WHERE TO STAY

The truth is there are not many good, value-for-money hotels available in Vajana and those few that do exist have suffered in recent years from rising prices and/or damp. Of course, many people arrive in Vajana by car and this also rates as one of your better accommodation options. Those on a very tight budget should remember that during summer **Vajana University** opens its doors to visitors, allowing them to rent a student room or, for that matter, a student, at significantly discounted rates. Other choices include the following:

$$$ Accommodation Luxury

The **Vajana Ritzzz Hotjl** is located right on the picturesque main square – a delight for guests but a shame for the square itself which is marred by the hotel's concrete-bunker design. Rooms at the back are described as 'Mountain View', which is only partially misleading in that they do overlook a mountain of crushed car bodies piled up at a nearby auto wreckers.

✉ 6 Platka dj Busjbusj
☎ 90 1196
✆ 90 1197
@ ritzzz@moldi.co.mv
🛏 50 🍴 ✑
🖪 DC, MC, V

Note: The friendly staff all speak a range of languages and it's worth asking for a room with a balcony; you won't get one but it will give them a chance to practise their English.

Watch out!
Due to erratic water pressure, guests in Vajana's top hotels are advised against using the bidets (*frekljsqirtz*). As one recent visitor pointed out, 'There's a fine line between personal hygiene and colonic irrigation.'

The Vajana Ritzzz Hotjl – what it lacks in old world charm it more than makes up for in concrete.

$$ Accommodation **Mid-Range**

The **Hotjl Ozjecmet** is nothing special to look at but you'll find good, comfortable rooms here for quite reasonable prices. The service is efficient if slightly on the 'forceful' side. One guest recently reported telling a housemaid they didn't want their bed turned down, only to have her return with several colleagues and forcibly remove the duvet. They then refused to leave until the complimentary chocolate was eaten.

✉ 78 Av Busjbusj
☎ 91 1961
🖷 91 1962
@ oz@molnet.co.mv
🗝34 🍴
▤MC, V

For the stressed-out traveller, consider booking a room at **Club Spza**, a funky new boutique hotel with an emphasis on relaxation. In addition to hot tubs and sauna rooms, a full range of massage services are offered, including remedial (non-sexual), deep tissue (non-sexual), sports injury (non-sexual) and erotic double lesbian topless (non-sexual).

✉ 54 Av Molvanja
☎ 94 8686
🖷 94 8687
@ spza@moldi.co.mv
🗝32
▤DC, MC, V

$ Accommodation **Budget**

In summer the **Vajana University's** dormitories are fumigated and opened up to visitors, providing a cheap alternative to hotels. Good value and hearty meals are also served in a temporary cafeteria set up at the rear of the university's veterinary school.

✉ 212 Sv St Fyodor
☎ 92 9575
🖷 92 9555
@ uni@molnet.co.mv
🗝302 🍴 ▤DC

Another good budget option is **Olga's**, a small private hostel run by the feisty Olga Kramcesvki, a Polish immigrant turned hotelier. Rooms here are small and facilities pretty basic but the prices are low and there's space to chill out in a shady terrace garden that, like the owner's armpits, is delightfully overgrown.

✉ 45 Av Molvanja
☎ 99 0343
@ olga@moldi.co.mv
🗝8
▤V

Traveller's Tip
In many of Vajana's less expensive hotels the breakfast facilities are self-serve. If planning to use the toaster, guests are advised to make sure they are wearing well-insulated footwear.

WHERE TO EAT

If you're after truly traditional Molvanian cooking then Vajana is the perfect place to enjoy a meal out. Here you'll find local specialities such as the popular **liver and giblet** combination *hercmec* (often served as dessert in a waffle cone), as well as *kvorvecz*, a thick, rich soup named after a former Vajana mayor who shared similar qualities. It's worth remembering that, whilst most restaurants in Vajana are licensed, several 'BYOs' are starting to spring up. At these establishments diners may bring their own wine but should expect to either pay a 20% corkage fee or, alternatively, allow the waiter to drink 20% of the bottle.

$$$ Dining Luxury

Close to the Town Hall you'll find **Tozi Rzal**, an old brick building with vaulted ceilings and terracotta floors. It is said that Prime Minister Busjbusj once threw up here. The emphasis is on elegance and the set menu includes a choice of several sumptuous main courses followed by a fruit sorbet, designed to help cleanse the palate in preparation for dessert which, unfortunately, also happens to be fruit sorbet.

✉ *10 Platka dj Busjbusj*
☎ *94 6866*
🏦 *DC, MC, V*

The **Vebrizic Bistroj** is one of Vajana's most famous eateries and for years diners have packed this busy first-floor restaurant to enjoy the spectacle of watching chefs prepare the local favourite, venison cooked in a flaming cognac sauce, served flamboyantly at the table on a sizzling plate. Sadly, the building burnt to the ground last year, but there are plans to re-build.

✉ *63 Av Busjbusj*
closed due to fire

$$ Dining Mid-Range

A slightly more casual eating institution is **Valgzos**, a *tavernja*-style bistro specializing in local dishes. Typical meals contain onion, garlic, chilli, paprika, cabbage and red lentils. Bookings are essential, as is a window seat.

✉ *32 Sv Puffnstuff*
☎ *93 6934*

$ Dining Budget

Visitors on the go might wish to grab a bite at one of Vajana's popular **Subwayz** outlets. Based heavily on the similar-sounding US chain (in fact, proceedings are still before the courts), these sandwich bars offer a wide range of filled rolls including a 'weight-watchers special' advertised as containing less than 600g of fat.

✉ *34 Sv Puffnstuff*
✉ *23 Av Busjbusj*
✉ *75 Sv Pinochet*

HIGHLIGHTS

Many visitors come all the way to Vajana simply to visit its famous **outdoor zoo**, and a quick stroll around this impressive facility will soon show you why. Set amid four hectares of lush gardens and ringed by electric fencing, the Vajana Zoo contains one of the largest collections of animals and birds in Eastern Europe. In fact, there are 2500 animals and 400 species in just over 65 cages, officially recognized as one of the **highest densities** of animal incarceration in the world.

One of the many exhibits at the Vajana Zoo is the Molvanian Spotted Tern, the only water bird in the world capable of breathing through its own anus.

The zoo is open daily 9am–4.30pm weekdays and on Fridays you can hear a talk from the resident veterinary pathologist explaining how each animal died that week.

Directly opposite the Town Hall is Vajana's **Museum of Medieval Dentistry** (*Muszm Dentjk Medjvl*). Tours of this fascinating, if somewhat macabre, facility are available weekdays and there is also a sound and video presentation that takes you through the history of early advances in oral hygiene. One visitor reported it was very informative but, at just over 150 minutes, perhaps a little too detailed, especially in the area of **inflammatory gum disease**.

To the north of the city you'll find the tranquil waters of **Lake Debrizca**, an impressive 134 hectare impoundment popular with local boat owners and families enjoying picnics. Tour buses also frequently stop here to pump out their on-board **toilet facilities** but, while you have to be careful, little can take away from this truly splendid setting. Various watersports are offered at the lake, including water-skiing, windsurfing and parascending, which has been described as a cross between hang-gliding and suicide.

Lake Debrizca was originally formed by glacial activity during the Ice Age (65 million years ago) and was then further enlarged during the Hydro-Electric Age (the 1950s).

Many people come to Vajana keen to purchase products made from Molvanian cedar, a highly sought-after wood, widely used by local craftsmen in furniture. Buyers should be advised, however, that whilst strong when first cut, **Molvanian cedar** easily splinters and cracks without warning. It is also the only timber in the world that rusts.

Vajana's famous Chateau Stencchberp.

Vajana is an historic wine-growing region and produces the world's only red Riesling. The most popular wine is a type of claret made out of a grape variety unique to this area called **Soursavignon**. Many wine writers struggle to describe the taste of this grape but most liken it to **fermented lemon rind**. The grape has an extremely tough skin and for many years could only be crushed by rifle butts. The grape juice from this crush is extremely astringent and must undergo a filter press. The first run-off is used in **premium cuvees** and the second juice is used to tan saddles.

Back to School...

When most people think of alternative teaching methods they think of Montessori or Steiner; however, Molvania has also pioneered its own system of early-learning, based around the writings of Vajana-born visionary V.Z. Vzeclep (1823–1878). **Vzeclep Instjtuts**, as they are known, can be found throughout the country and are built around an educational philosophy known as *Ne Drabjovit Vard Szlabo* (literally, 'don't beat the donkey too hard'). This system of teaching places a great emphasis on both posture and breathing, and children at Vzeclep Schools spend the first six years of their student life strapped in specially-designed harnesses.

The class of '52. Happy pupils of the first Vzeclep School enjoy their weekly recess break.

THE POSTENWALJ RANGES

One of the most famous tourist attractions in southern Molvania can be found just a few hundred kilometres east of Svetranj, the beautiful Postenwalj Ranges. This heavily-wooded mountain region, popular with hikers, skiers and those searching for unmarked graves, was declared a **national park** in 1965. A few years later it was declared a disaster zone after an agricultural fertilizer spill upstream on the **River Vzintga** threatened to wipe out all wildlife – but since that time extensive efforts have gone into restoring the area to its original beauty. Being so popular, the park naturally gets a little crowded, especially on weekends when members of the **Svetranj Gun Club** take to the hills for

Since the installation of extensive snow making facilities, the Postenwalj Ranges have become a ski lover's paradise, offering extensive, well-groomed runs on a firm base of basalt.

target practice. During these times visitors are advised to wear bright clothes and avoid looking like a moose or gypsy labourer.

Lights, Action, Camera!

As any local will tell you, the Postenwalj Ranges almost reached world prominence a few years back when producers of the American reality TV program 'Survivor' decided to film a series here. What was hoped to be a major boost for tourism turned sour, however, when taping was cancelled after several members of one tribe accidentally stood on an unexploded land-mine during the first immunity challenge.

GETTING THERE

The Ranges are linked to Svetranj and Vajana by local buses; however, their frequency depends on the season and mood of the drivers. There is also a **tunnel** through the mountains to Hungary, although it's often closed for repairs or rescue efforts.

Important road signs in the Postenwalj Ranges

STEEP SLOPE

VERY STEEP SLOPE

WALL

WHERE TO STAY

Just past the main entrance to the Postenwalj National Park is a magnificent 17th century **chateau** that once belonged to the Duke of Svetranj (who went on to become King Prablik the Quarrelsome). It's now open to the public as a hotel and also contains a small cafe where light meals are served. In addition there is a 'museum', although one reader advised us this establishment was little more than an over-priced gift shop whose only **antiquities** appeared to be its selection of pastries as well as a few old fridge magnets. You enter the chateau across a bridge which spans a pit holding several **bears**. A sign warns visitors of the danger of getting too close to these bears – they have no teeth or claws but do carry a highly transmittable form of mange.

✉ *11 Sv Busjbusj*
☎ *99 9996*
🖷 *99 9997*
🛏 *14* 🍽 ✏
▤ *DC, MC, V*

On an even more opulent scale is the magnificent **Vilja Posten** where former Prime Minister Busjbusj once hosted numerous members of European royalty. This historic residence, set on six hectares of gardens at the foot of the Ranges, was converted into a **boutique hotel** in 1983 and became part of the World Luxury Hotels Association in 1985. It remained so until 1992 when it was discovered no such organization existed.

✉ *63 Sv Busjbusj*
☎ *99 6427*
🖷 *99 6428*
@ *posten@moldi.co.mv*
🛏 *50* 🍽
▤ *DC*

Note: Rooms are large and have a good range of facilities, including hair-dryers and large safes that could, at a pinch, double as a child's room.

On a slightly less opulent note, visitors planning to base themselves in the Postenwalj region might consider a night or two at the **Jzuckblec Manor**. This cosy B&B was originally a farmhouse, which could well explain the smell of animal dung permeating the rooms – but it remains a delightful alternative to the more upmarket accommodation on offer.

✉ *59 Sv Busjbusj*
☎ *99 6623*
🖷 *jzuck@moldi.co.mv*
🛏 *13*
▤ *DC*

WHERE TO EAT

Not far from the entrance to the Postenwalj National Park in the delightful hamlet of Arjenspak you'll find **Gostinka Lec**, a traditional trattoria-style restaurant where everything served is grown in the proprietor's very own vegetable garden. Start off with a bowl of hearty zucchini soup followed by zucchini roulade served on a bed of zucchini fritters and washed down with a glass of sparkling zucchini beer. Or, for a change, try the '**pork surprise**' (it's made out of zucchini).

✉ *11 Sv Liski*
☎ *99 0996*

Meanwhile, in the neighbouring village of Tzujek you'll find **Mzino**, a friendly bistro popular with travellers en route to the mountains. The house speciality here is black pudding and turnips, while many enjoy the Mzino plate, a mixed platter of **barbecued meats** served on rice. There is also a children's menu, consisting of pretty much the same fare to which brightly coloured food dyes are added.

✉ *51 Sv Liski*
☎ *99 8535*

Philippe writes...

❝*Why pay for a bland, westernized meal in an overpriced tourist cafe when, for half the cost, a street vendor will sell you a piece of salted cod and a bag of lemon rind?* ❞   *P.M.*

When dining in certain parts of southern Molvania it is considered rude to ask for cutlery.

HIGHLIGHTS

Hiking is enormously popular in the Postenwalj Ranges and there are numerous places of interest for the intrepid traveller to explore.

The **Vzintga Gorge** was cut between precipitous cliffs by the powerful River Vzintga, which flows down numerous **pools and waterfalls**. There is a marked trail to the top of the gorge where the views are quite outstanding. Sadly, the spectacular cable-car that once carried visitors across the gorge no longer operates, but you can still see the old pylons and engine-house as well as view a **memorial plaque** dedicated to the service's last 23 passengers.

Bzejenko Lec (Lake Bzejenko) is nestled within a rim of mountains and surrounded by spruce forests, with a castle on one side and a promenade beneath stately chestnut trees on the other. Standing by the water's edge it would be easy to imagine you were back in the 17th century, were it not for the regular presence of the **Postenwalj Jet Ski Club** who hold numerous events on this inland waterway.

We Were Wrong! In a previous edition the forests to the north of Lake Bzejenko were described as being one of the 'least explored' regions in southern Molvania. This was a typographical error; they are, in fact, one of the 'least-exploded' regions.

Soaking it in...

If all this hiking, skiing and riding sounds a little energetic, don't forget that the ranges are also home to one of the most magnificently situated spa resorts in Europe. The healing powers of the **thermal springs** at Drypp have been known since the Middle Ages and even today visitors come to enjoy the benefit of these miraculous waters. These unusually acidic springs are particularly renowned for their dermatological effect, curing ailments of the skin by stripping much of it from the body. Many of the thermal pools in this region are privately owned and the best way to enjoy them is by booking into a spa complex such as the **Jredvej Thermjka**, where you can soak in a therapeutic pool for hours. One fee covers your admission, towel, locker and complimentary fungal foot powder.

During the winter months the Postenwalj Ranges attract skiers from all over Europe. The most popular resort is located on **Mount Zacwcej**, which offers a good range of slopes to suit beginners and veterans alike. A special feature of Mount Zacwcej is the fact it offers **night skiing**, courtesy of large floodlights originally installed to prevent disgruntled Slovakian resort staff from escaping back to their families.

Many well-established **cycling paths** pass through the lower ranges, however, finding a place to hire a bike can be difficult. The *Ztumcej Tavernja* in nearby **Tzujek** will rent you one but the owner insists on accompanying all riders and he's quite heavy.

Holy Water!
Visitors to the Postenwalj Ranges will at some time or other be offered a glass of *Karolcyi*, a sweet liqueur produced by local Brigidine Monks and manufactured to a secret recipe purportedly dating back to the Middle Ages. However, this claim was called into question recently when a former member of the order, Brother Vedjuz, confessed on a national current affairs program that the drink was largely made from ethanol and cough mixture. Strangely, this revelation has not affected sales.

Despite being just 700m high the Postenwalj Ranges attract skiers from all over Molvania.

The price of using ski lifts can be greatly reduced by carrying several family members on the one ticket.

Bardjov

Lake Mzaukera

River Uze

•Dzrebo

•Lublova

Lake Skrotul

EASTERN
STEPPES

River Fiztula

Bzejenko

THE EASTERN STEPPES

[Stjppka Orjentlka]

THE REGION

Perhaps the first thing that strikes visitors to Molvania's eastern districts is the colours: lush greens, earthen browns and bright, rich yellows all burst in dazzling glory from the teeth of local residents tucked away in this **isolated** part of the country. Whilst the east of Molvania may not abound in **natural beauty** or civic treasures there is much here to enjoy for the savvy traveller prepared to look beyond the **bleak** post-war cities and de-forested hills. Indeed, each year more and more people are visiting the Eastern Steppes region – either on organized tours or as part of refugee resettlement programs – and discovering **hidden gems** amongst the drab Communist-era architecture and pockets of heavy pollution. There are beautifully historic cities like **Bardjov**, thought to have once been mentioned by Shakespeare himself:

> *'Curs'd dominion foul poxen lair*
> *Where misery meet with fortune grim*
> *And drab spirit doth blight the soul*
> *Across the blasted plain...'*

Outside the cities there is also much to recommend this area in the way of natural beauty, such as the magnificent wild lake lands of **Mzaukera**, where each year wild teal geese return from their 10,000km migratory voyage to nest and be shot at. Meanwhile, a little south are the beautiful **Pucjicj Hills** where keen hikers can walk for miles without seeing so much as a road or electricity pylon, provided of course they do it at night.

Because of its isolation, the east of Molvania has developed a unique culture that is reflected in a variety of ways. Its folk music, for example, with its emphasis on volume over melody, is heard nowhere but here. The local cuisine is also distinctive, drawing heavily as it does on the silverbeet. Even the **regional dialect** remains exclusive to the east, with simple greetings such as *ercj Djeum a vrozem-krum* (literally, 'may God inseminate your wife'). But, of course, it is these very differences that make a visit to the exotic east so worthwhile.

Traveller's Tip
Whilst the younger generation are less concerned with traditions, in outlying areas of the east the people are noticeably conservative and care should be taken to avoid offence by wearing skimpy clothes, displaying open signs of affection or referring to the earth as being anything other than flat.

Eastern Molvanian men play Rubrav, *a popular card game similar to 'strip poker' except that, instead of removing clothes, losing bidders must don table napkins.*

BARDJOV

Bardjov (pronounced 'Bardy-ce-jzoff') is one of the largest and most vibrant cities in eastern Molvania. Apart from being a cultural and historical capital, 70% of the country's **cement** is quarried here. Situated on the exposed plains of the Molvanian tundra, Bardjov suffers frequently from the strong Bora winds that sweep in from the east. Ever resourceful, the local government decided to capitalize on this year-round phenomenon by setting up a **wind farm** on the city's outskirts. However, regrettably, three of the four massive turbines actually blew over, preventing the ambitious project from ever realising its full potential. Due to these winds and poor farming practices the entire area is virtually devoid of vegetation, yet it is this very barrenness that lends a special charm to this provincial outpost.

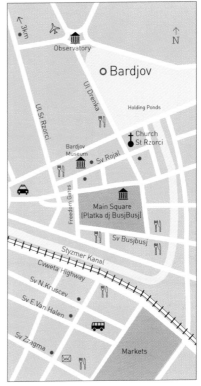

HISTORY

Inhabited at various times by a mix of Slovak, Croatian and Hungarian tribes, it was **Zjabdre I** (1609–1665), the first Duke of Bardjov, who realized that the only way to bring peace to his kingdom would be by uniting the various warring factions through marriage. To this end, he arranged for his half-Prussian son **Leostk** to marry the grand-daughter of Slovakian **Emperor Theuzdo** and his Budapest-born wife **Zzagma** in the hope they would produce an heir to unite the region. Instead, Zzagma poisoned her husband at the wedding feast and stole the gifts before declaring war on the city. Internal conflicts continued to rage for decades before Bardjov fell under the control of the **Zvetmir dynasty**. Although at times cruel, this ruling family introduced stability to the region (as well as **late-night shopping**) and are still remembered with an annual holiday on which locals enjoy elaborate picnics, and municipal jails are thrown open.

SHOPPING

Bardjov, due to its position as a regional centre of contraband, is a wonderful town to engage in a bit of 'retail therapy' and, as you wander through its many shops and market stalls, you will regularly hear the familiar tap-tap-tap of chisels on brass. Often this is just a **dentist** plying his trade, but sometimes you will be lucky enough to come across a genuine artisan applying the finishing touches to an ashtray, name-plate or set of drinking goblets. Stylish clothes are the other big seller in Bardjov and the savvy shopper can easily come home with an entire wardrobe of last year's fashions. **Leather goods** are also a great surprise – not only are they cheap, they're made from vinyl.

HOW TO GET THERE

Although not technically a stop, the main Lutenblag–Bratislava train regularly breaks down in Bardjov, affording the intrepid traveller a marvellous opportunity to explore the city. You can also drive from Lutenblag on the **Cvweta Highway**, although be aware that this is a very rough road and because of its many narrow, exposed curves and steep sections it should only be attempted in a well-maintained vehicle driven by a safe, experienced driver. This pretty much rules out all Molvanian buses.

HOW TO GET AROUND

The public transport system in Bardjov can best be described as 'challenging' with buses and trains notoriously unreliable. Without doubt the best means of getting around is taxi. By law, cab drivers must use their meters. Unfortunately, no such obligation relates to them using their indicators or deodorant. On a reassuring note, all cabs operating in the Bardjov city region are fitted with **security screens** that completely surround the driver and make it virtually impossible for passengers to be attacked by him.

Ooh-la-la! Bardjov fashion designers specialize in jackets made entirely out of recycled car seats.

WHERE TO STAY

The adoption of a standard accommodation **star rating system** has not been uniform across Molvania and here in Bardjov it can be particularly misleading. For example, a rating of 'five' could well indicate luxurious features combined with **elegant surrounds**, but is just as likely to be a reference to the number of working toilets in the hotel. The best advice is to inspect any establishment before booking a room. Outside the city your accommodation options are a little more limited, although there are quite a few new B&B's (Bed and Brandy) establishments open for bookings.

$$$ Accommodation Luxury

At the top end you can't go past **Hotjl Palfvi** on the north-west corner of Szerti Platka. It's a 250-year-old Carmelite convent that has been tastefully restored with a real eye to period detail. For example, each room features a large wooden crucifix that opens to reveal a fully-stocked mini-bar. All the luxuries you'd expect from a five-star hotel are here, such as air-conditioning and cable TV, although caution should be exercised when using the electric spa-bath as much of the wiring is visibly faulty. In fact, a small sign above the pumping mechanism warns it must not be operated without a uniformed member of the local fire brigade in attendance.

✉ *55 Sv Rojal*
☎ *74 3805*
℻ *74 3815*
@ *palfvi@molnet.co.mv*
🛏 *46* 🍴 ✎
▤ *DC, MC, V*

Another centrally-located hotel is the large **Istvan Hozceski**, opposite the Bardjov Museum. The foyer is clean and bright with freshly-cut flowers and plenty of light. Unfortunately, it's all downhill from here as the rest of the place is decorated in dull shades of brown and green which, while not offering much in the way of visual beauty, at least match the colour of the water in the hotel's swimming pool. Staff are attentive, although the service can be a little brusque. One traveller reported asking the concierge where he could find a non-smoking room, only to be informed 'Austria'.

✉ *78 Sv Rojal*
☎ *71 4021*
℻ *71 4022*
@ *istvan@moldi.co.mv*
🛏 *56* 🍴 ✎
▤ *DC, MC, V*

Visitor's Note *Due to the extraordinary amount of building work and refurbishment currently being undertaken in and around Bardjov, municipal officials have taken the unprecedented step of declaring the entire city a construction site and visitors are required to wear a hard hat at all times.*

$$ Accommodation **Mid-Range**

A good mid-priced option is the recently-opened **Vja Zac**. The rooms here are plain and simple, as are most of the staff, and there are good stand-by rates if you're prepared to wait for a cancellation or sudden death. Being so close to the centre of town, traffic noise in some rooms can be rather intrusive when the windows are open, but fortunately this is not a major problem as very few of the windows actually open.

✉ 12 Sv N.Kruscev
☎ 78 9696
🖷 78 9690
@ zac@moldi.co.mv
🔑 20 🍴 ✐
🗏 DC, MC, V

Opposite the bus station is one of Bardjov's newest hotel complexes, the six-storey **Holidaj Injn**. Like the US chain, the emphasis here is on consistency, and management have made sure that all the rooms feature thin walls, non-functioning toilets and a lingering smell of stale cigar smoke. The hotel also boasts a 'Leisure Club' ('*Klub Lezur*') but this would appear to be little more than a partially carpeted room with a half-sized billiard table and a deck of cards.

✉ 123 Sv E.Van Halen
☎ 74 2123
🖷 74 2122
@ holi@molnet.co.mv
🔑 90 🍴 ✐
🗏 DC, MC, V

$ Accommodation **Budget**

Bardjov offers a wide range of budget-style accommodation, perhaps the best of which is a small, private hostel at **10 Zzagma**. There are no signs outside except a small one on the doorbell reading *Bzekevak* ('Condemned') and, like much of the accommodation in Bardjov, rooms can be rented here by either the day or the hour, depending on your risk profile.

✉ 10 Sv Zzagma
☎ 79 7050
🔑 12
🗏 MC, V

The **Bardjov Youth Hostel** is popular with backpackers and students or those seeking to chat them up. The dormitories here are all single-sex (meaning you can only have sex once a day) and there is an aggressively enforced 10pm curfew.

✉ 32 Sv Rojal
☎ 76 6023
@ youth@moldi.co.mv
🔑 98
🗏 DC, MC, V

Camping is not recommended in Bardjov due to the difficulty of keeping a tent upright in high winds; however, small cabins can be rented in the **Tzeodram Kravci**, a tourist park some 3km north-west of town. The accommodation is pretty basic but it's cheap – S120 per night (S150 with a roof) – and the park provides good views out over the adjacent limestone quarry.

✉ 264 Ul St Rzorci
☎ 71 1236
🔑 6

WHERE TO EAT

Don't expect gastronomic delights in Bardjov as the choices, especially in outlying regions, are usually limited to roast pork with parsnip and **dumplings**. If this fare gets a little monotonous after a few weeks and you want a real change you might try asking for no dumplings – but do expect to pay extra. Another feature likely to inflate any restaurant bill is the high cost of quality imported wines, which are very expensive in Bardjov due to the fact that they are taxed as luxury items, along with tobacco and **antibiotics**.

$$$ Dining Luxury

For many years the most popular dining establishment in Bardjov has been **Zoycvejs**, a meat and seafood bistro opposite the city's cathedral. The signature dish here used to be the flaming grill in which a variety of meats were cooked at the table on a portable gas stove. Sadly, it burnt down in 1999, but a replacement **Zoycvejs II** is now operating. (Open Tuesday–Sunday, closed Monday, Wednesday and days of total fire ban.)

✉ *51 Sv Rojal*
☎ *79 2692*
▭ *MC, V*

Another centrally located eatery is **Cafe Dragjec**. Locals claim this is the best place to dine in Bardjov. Avoid it at all costs.

✉ *89 Sv Rojal*
☎ *74 9898*

A short walk from the post office down Bzecvec Ulijca will take you to **Bistroj Zjekl**, a cosy, relaxed restaurant that specializes in game dishes. Try the rare roasted pork, stewed hare in cream sauce or the squirrel terrine.

✉ *42 Sv Zzagma*
☎ *73 2834*

Mule testicles hang from a tree. Once dried, they will be either turned into a child's toy or served as luncheon meat in one of Bardjov's many restaurants.

$$ Dining **Mid-Range**

Try soaking in a bit of local colour at the popular and often crowded **Wjikic** bar and bistro just off Sv. Marji. The atmosphere here is casual, as is the staff's approach to personal hygiene, but the meals are generally good. Described as 'nouveau Molvanian' the emphasis is not so much on freshness or flavour but quantity. Try their famous herring in mushroom sauce – one of the more unusual desserts you're likely to encounter.

✉ *64 Sv Busjbusj*
☎ *71 3211*

We Were Wrong! Our last edition contained a reference to a popular local cafe that should have read 'Bardjov diners are always welcome in **Maria's Brasserie**'. They are not, to the best of our knowledge, welcome in her 'Brassiere'. We apologise to Maria for any offence, hurt or overcrowding this error may have caused.

$ Dining **Budget**

'Pitsa Parlours' are becoming increasingly popular in downtown Bardjov and one of the newest is **Zjippy's**, a relaxed eatery popular with students and homeless men. Although a limited delivery service is available to surrounding hotels, due to unreliable transport vehicles your order may often arrive the following day. But don't despair – even cold, the pizzas here are delicious!

✉ *4 Sv Busjbusj*
☎ *77 0938*

Just off Bardjov's main square you will find the surprisingly affordable **Vjed Jbec** bistro. There is an extensive menu and you can't go wrong with the food here, unless you try eating it. Some of the meals can be a little on the heavy side but, one way or another, they're not likely to be in your stomach for long.

✉ *21 Sv Busjbusj*
☎ *78 5246*

Not for the Faint-Hearted!

Visitors to Bardjov will at one point or other be offered a piece of *muczecl*, a traditional shepherd's cheese produced from goat's milk. What makes this delicacy somewhat unique, apart from its pungent aroma and repugnant flavour, is that the cheese itself is infested with live maggots. Many travellers find this feature somewhat off-putting, if not downright shocking, but after a few weeks of dining in Molvania, it's a phenomenon you're likely to become well and truly acquainted with. One word of caution: *muczecl* is not recommended for anyone with diabetes or a heart condition. It's also been known to induce women to go into labour – even those who weren't pregnant.

HIGHLIGHTS

A popular pastime for visitors to Bardjov is taking a *zwak* (Molvanian gondola) along the **Styzmer Kanal**, Eastern Europe's largest inland sewerage channel. A leisurely trip from the city centre through to the holding ponds takes about three hours, depending on flows at the water treatment pumping station.

The **Bardjov Museum** is a large building near the centre of town featuring a significant collection of Molvanian treasures and relics. You could easily spend a day here: one or two hours touring the **exhibits** and the rest of your time queuing for the museum's one and only toilet. Don't be discouraged though – this museum is well worth your effort and inconvenience.

Roll Up! Roll Up!

The Royal Molvanian Circus features jugglers, trapeze artists, goat-tamers, performing rats, strippers (evening sessions only) and the spectacular barefoot horse riders of Lublova. All this, capped off by the drunken antics of Molestov the Klown, makes it one of the most memorable experiences you'll ever have under canvas.

Despite being a little out of town, the **Crkja St Rzorci** (Church of St Rzorci) is a must-see for any visitor to Bardjov. The church itself is an interesting mix of Gothic, Baroque and fibro-cement building styles and houses numerous works of major artistic merit. The ceiling of the church features **barrel vaulting** and is covered in panels depicting various biblical events. Sadly, the city-founders ran short of money and these panels were never completely finished; however, visitors can still marvel at the intricate brushwork contained in such significant scenes as *The Two Wise Men* and *Christ Praying with his Nine Apostles.*

Party Time! A local Barjovian celebrates National Fertility Day, marking the date Viagra was introduced into Molvania as an over-the-counter drug.

The massive bronze **Freedom Gates** (*Libertjolkas*) at the entrance to Bardjov's main square bear the inscription 'Peace, Harmony and Love' and were presented as a gift to the city by occupying Nazi forces in 1942.

Star Struck!
A few kilometres to the north of the city you'll find the **Bardjov Observatory** (*Observaltrisko*), a 140m radio telescope facility capable of detecting faint signals from deep space. Up until the 1980s this observatory was part of NASA's SETI program. Sadly, these days, due to funding cut-backs, it is used mainly to pick up and re-transmit the EuroPorn cable TV network across eastern Molvania.

A real attraction for visitors to Bardjov is the **Old Palace**, which can be found just north of the **Styzmer Kanal**. First built in 1431, then expanded over the next 400 years, the Palace was badly damaged by fire in 1864 and then re-built, only to suffer a direct hit from German artillery during World War II. Fortunately, the Palace's carvings, chandeliers, antiques and artwork had all been removed for safe-keeping. Unfortunately, they'd been removed to **Russia** and have not been seen since.

Automotive Excellence
Visitors to Bardjov will no doubt wish to visit the extensive automotive factory to the north of town where Molvania's national car, the Skumpta, is manufactured. This functional vehicle may appear unorthodox to western eyes, with its single headlamp, three cylinders and candlelit interior, but the proof is in the pudding and it has proved remarkably durable, so much so that owners are required by law to install odometers that record up to 10,000,000 kilometres. The Skumpta has scored well in recent safety tests that involved four leading European car models being driven into a wall at 60kmh. The other three suffered extensive front-end damage whereas the Skumpta emerged unscathed, having broken down every time during the run up.

A Survivor's Tale...
For many people Bardjov will forever be associated with the remarkable story of Lt Vladko, a Molvanian soldier who, in 1945, was found by Russian soldiers in the forest south of this remote village. Thinking World War II was still going, Vladko gave himself up to his captors. It *was* still going and he was shot for collaborating with the enemy.

LUBLOVA

Lacking the stark natural beauty of villages to the west, Lublova still has much to offer the intrepid traveller prepared to negotiate the difficult journey across the barren plateau to this fascinating **frontier town**. Here you'll find yourself back in the Middle Ages, certainly in terms of transport and accommodation, surrounded by **olde worlde charm** at every turn. Yes, parts of the modern city are less

than attractive, with their jumble of factories and high-rise apartment blocks, but the funny thing about Lublova is that just when you're about to despair you'll come around a corner and see a church or hidden town square that will take your breath away. Speaking of pollution, the city authorities have gone to considerable lengths in their battle to improve Lublova's general **air quality**. To this end, diesel generators and coal stoves may now only be operated between the hours of 6am and midnight. Despite these drastic measures the Old Town's face has been irreparably stained by emissions from the nearby steelworks in the outlying suburb of **Drabb**.

These days Lublova is perhaps best known as the location of **Molvania's largest university** (*Unjverstad Nazjonal*). Students and researchers come from all over Europe to study at its prestigious **medical school**, drawn by its reputation for academic excellence, coupled with liberal attitudes towards embryonic stem cell research.

Research facilities at Lublova's medical school are amongst some of the finest in Eastern Europe.

Star Pupil!

Lublova University's most famous son, Antonin Vlatvja, studied here from 1491 to 1495. A keen astronomer, he would gaze at the heavens through a long tubular device he called a *tojlet rol*. Vlatvja has been widely acknowledged as the first scientist to hypothesise that, rather than the sun revolving round the earth, the earth in fact revolves around Neptune. Of course, such outrageous claims did not exactly go unnoticed and in 1496 Vlatvja was called before a Papal inquiry in Rome where charges of heresy were dropped. He was, however, condemned to death as an idiot.

HISTORY

Lublova enjoys a long history as an important frontier town and the cultural centre of eastern Molvania. Originally inhabited by Illyrian and Celtic tribes, it later came to serve as an important commercial centre, a role maintained today with over 80% of Molvania's illegal

arms trade being conducted within the city. In 1396 Lublova was conquered by **King Svardo III** ('The Dwarf King') of Croatia, who later gave the town to his son and daughter-in-law as a wedding present. They decided to exchange it for a **fortified village** further north and Lublova remained without a clear ruler for several hundred years. Between 1603 and 1622, in response to a threat of invasion by the **Tatars**, the whole city was enclosed within a 2.4km-long wall. Unfortunately, the builders left a 1.8km-wide gap at the back and the entire town was razed by foreign invaders, before being extensively rebuilt during the 18th century.

With its story-book streets, Renaissance arcades and enchanting architecture, Lublova is one of the few Molvanian cities to escape devastation by Hitler's armies during World War II. Tragically though, much of the city was subsequently destroyed by fire in 1945 when an **Armistice Day** celebratory bonfire got out of hand. However, many **landmarks** remain unscathed and Lublovans hold great pride in their historic past. Nowhere is this more evident than on the beautifully preserved *Svej Rojal* or 'Royal Way', a magnificent promenade that is walked each year by the Prince of Lublova on the anniversary of his coronation. These days the incumbent Prince is forced to make the trip in a **fork-lift** due to chronic gout, but the locals' love of pomp and pageantry remains as strong as ever.

Philippe writes...

" *The fact is, you see nothing from a motorway, and I'm always bemused by tourists who think they're experiencing a country when all they're doing is heading down a highway in some luxury coach. I once travelled from Lublova to Dzrebo along a disused goat track that wound its way right over the Jikbenmar Mountains. The journey took us through some of the most spectacular and*  *beautiful landscapes in the world and, had the heavy blanket of fog ever lifted, I would have had some pretty special memories.* " P.M.

SHOPPING

Lublova's oldest department store Uzkro has a monumental staircase, Art Nouveau stained-glass windows and elaborately decorated counters. Sadly, it is virtually devoid of **merchandise**, unless you're after socks or storage jars. Uzkro is, however, one of the few places in Molvania to still sell the locally manufactured **Vzoykcle** computer systems. Designed and built right here in Lublova at the height of the 1980s IT boom, the Vzoykcle struggled to capture a large share of the home computer market due, in part, to its excessively **noisy internal fan** that, at levels of 120db, meant the unit could only be safely operated by those wearing hearing protection. To further complicate matters, the hard-drive also had a clutch. But complete systems (computer, software, ear-muffs) are still available at quite reasonable prices.

The other bargain to be found in Lublova is dental work, provided at cut-price rates by students from the local university. This service is very popular with Romanian tourists who come across on specially organized '**bridge and crown tours**', so it's worth booking ahead.

HOW TO GET THERE

Bus The trip by bus from Lutenblag to Lublova can be a bone-jarring experience, thanks not only to the **poor quality** of the roads, but also the somewhat curious tendency of local transport operators to save money by cutting back on the amount of air used in their tyres.

Train There is a 'scenic' train from Bardjov to Lublova that passes through the panoramic **Jzerckev National Park**; however, visitors keen to enjoy the views should be warned that for much of this section of the journey the train travels through an underground tunnel.

Air Whilst there is an airport in Lublova it is classified by civil aviation authorities as 'Category D', making it suitable for emergency landings only. Built on less than a hectare of land it actually features one of the only curved runways in the world.

HOW TO GET AROUND

Taxis used to be a nightmare throughout the Eastern Steppes region but are now properly regulated. In Lublova all cabs must be licensed and **fumigated** at least once a month. Drivers are also obliged to have their photo ID on constant display, showing name, licence number and proof they've recently attended an anger management class.

Trollejbuses (trolley buses) run frequently and are the fastest means of public transport, since they are not affected by traffic hold-ups. They are, however, affected by **armed hold-ups** on a depressingly regular basis and commuters should be wary about carrying large sums of money or young children.

WHERE TO STAY

Choices of accommodation in Lublova have been a little more limited since the opulent **Tvorz Grand Hotjl** burnt down in 1998 after a trouser press caught fire. However, there are several good options still available in a variety of price categories.

$$$ Accommodation Luxury

Just off the main square in the Old Town you will find the impressive **Hotjl Fzor Ztejl**, a grand establishment of some six storeys. The 'Ztej', as it is affectionately known, has everything you'd expect from a luxury hotel with the possible exception of reliable plumbing and a lift. Most of the rooms feature sweeping views of the apartment block next door.

✉ *12 Av Busjbusj*
☎ *62 3524*
🖷 *62 3525*
@ *fzor@molnet.co.mv*
🛏 *60* 🍴 🖉
▤ *DC, MC, V*

Note: There is also a roof-top garden where guests can relax next to a large display of Molvanian thistles.

Just on the northern outskirts of the Old Town you'll find **Djabgor Lodge**, a large hotel popular with business travellers and tourists alike. Despite its somewhat 'olde worlde' appearance the building is not all that old and was only turned into a hotel in 1997. Prior to that it was used as a refugee detention centre and a lot of the security staff from those days seem to have stayed on (don't even *think* about stealing a bathrobe).

✉ *104 Sv Vladko*
☎ *62 5830*
🖷 *62 5830*
@ *djabor@moldi.co.mv*
🛏 *48* 🍴 🖉
▤ *DC, MC, V*

Note: The Lodge has its own Italian-style restaurant called 'Bella Vista', an interesting name given it is located in a basement.

Hotjl Pensjon Echzo on Sv. Strezmo promotes itself as a 'family' hotel, which is somewhat at odds with its round-the-clock gambling hall, topless bar and complete absence of non-smoking rooms. Echzo is, however, one of the few hotels in Lublova to offer a babysitting service, with children taken care of by the hour, evening or entire year, depending on your needs.

✉ *132 Sv Strezmo*
☎ *61 7905*
🖷 *62 5830*
@ *echzo@moldi.co.mv*
🛏 *32* 🍴 🖉
▤ *DC, MC, V*

Creepy-Crawly Alert!

Visitors to the far east of Molvania should keep an eye out for the horn-tailed spider, an eight-legged pest unique to this part of the world. These highly venomous creatures are attracted to cold, damp conditions where they can hide beneath rotting wood, which means you'll often find them in Lublova hotel rooms.

$$ | Accommodation **Mid-Range**

A short walk from Lublova's main railway station will take you to the modestly-priced **Cborej Bcej** hotel. There's nothing wrong with this large, modern 80-bedroom complex except for the fact it only has 14 beds. It also boasts a 'Conference Centre', although one business traveller reported this amounted to little more than a trestle table, five chairs and a broken overhead projector.

✉ *98 Sv Frortunju*
☎ *61 1196*
🖷 *61 1197*
@ *cborej@moldi.co.mv*
🗝 *80*
🛏 *V*

Despite being a little out of town, **Hotjl Kjonopist** offers good basic accommodation in a relaxed atmosphere. As a bonus the owner even speaks a few words of English (he grew up in Glasgow) and the rooms are large enough to contain a bed, armchair and desk, provided they're stacked on top of each other.

✉ *141 Sv Vladko*
☎ *69 6776*
🖷 *69 6777*
@ *kpist@molnet.co.mv*
🗝 *30*
🛏 *DC, MC*

$ | Accommodation **Budget**

Opened in 1995 and just under a kilometre to Lublova's city centre, the **Trizcejem Dormitorj** is actually run by a peasants' cooperative, and from the look of the rooms it has been decorated by one too. The carpets and walls are a uniformly drab brown with the only splashes of colour coming from the odd blood stain on the ceilings.

✉ *87 Ul St Gzemgrjo*
☎ *67 4038*
@ *triz@molnet.co.mv*
🗝 *24*
🛏 *DC, MC, V*

Note: Although the hotel claims to offer 'disabled access', one visitor reported that the wheelchair ramps on offer were so steep that anyone attempting to use them, if not completely disabled, would soon be rendered so.

The medium-sized **Pensjon Slobzan** is conveniently located near the museum and is popular with travellers who have limited budgets or expectations. This hotel has a family feel – it's crowded, noisy and there are frequent arguments about whose turn it is to put the rubbish out – but its central location means it is often booked out. The rooms are snug and clean, with wooden floors and pillows.

✉ *64 Sv Rojal*
☎ *65 3937*
@ *slobz@moldi.co.mv*
🗝 *55*
🛏 *MC, V*

Private **chatas** (cabins) may be rented in any of Lublova's many camping grounds; however, guests are advised to make sure that all rooms have been thoroughly sprayed for scorpions before moving in.

WHERE TO EAT

On 1 January 2002 the Lublova City Council introduced a non-smoking policy in all city restaurants. This was repealed at 7.30pm the following day in the wake of widespread **civil unrest** and has been replaced with a more relaxed and popular set of guidelines that basically permits diners to smoke provided that their chef is also doing so.

$$$ Dining Luxury

At the culinary top end of town you can't go past **Zjez Zjez**, one of Lublova's oldest and most prestigious dining establishments. The owners of this famous restaurant proudly boast that it was once visited by British Prime Minister Tony Blair. While this is technically true, they fail to mention he was visiting as part of an EU Parliamentary Delegation looking into the likely sources of the 2001 foot and mouth disease outbreak.

✉ *42 Av Nazjonal*
☎ *63 6937*
🖦 *DC, MC, V*

Bistroj Dezjamic is an older-style establishment on the main street. It was purchased in 2002 by a French restaurateur and food-lover whose first move was to close it down. (It is expected to re-open within 12 months.)

✉ *76 Av Busjbusj*
   currently closed

Backing onto the busy town square you'll find **Vadjroza**, a popular bistro that offers good food in what they describe as 'a relaxed, unhurried atmosphere' – meaning that there's only ever three waiters serving up to 100 diners. Dancing is popular here on weekends with exuberant male patrons showing off their prowess by making athletic leaps, slapping their heels in mid-air and rupturing ligaments in a frenzied display of misguided machismo.

✉ *6 Platka dj Busjbusj*
☎ *69 3757*
🖦 *DC, V*

Top Tip!
Many visitors to Lublova are keen to eat at its famous **Revolving Restaurant** but are unable to do so due to the high cost of this luxurious establishment. A good alternative is **Cafe Bgokcez**, where, after a few glasses of their house wine, you'll at least *feel* like you're in a revolving restaurant.

$$ Dining **Mid-Range**

Two blocks back from the museum on Sv. Strezmo you'll find the **Kaujcec Kjem**, a moderately-priced ground floor restaurant serving traditional and modern dishes. Very few of the underpaid and over-worked staff here speak English, which is just as well, as much of their cursing is best left untranslated.

✉ *88 Sv Strezmo*
☎ *67 7437*

Walk into **Kafe Udzrum** diagonally opposite the Post Office and you'll be immediately struck by the ornate light fixtures, so duck your head. Garishly bright tablecloths add to the complete mish-mash of interior decorating styles. But if the decor seems over-the-top, wait for the food. Large serves of heavily-salted meat floating in fat make this dining establishment a weight-watcher's nightmare. Described as 'hearty and heavy', the 'Udz' is one of the few places in Europe where it's possible to order a deep-fried salad.

✉ *67 Sv Vladko*
☎ *61 9077*

For those after authentic Lublovan fare, try the **Tzabian Jceje**. At this rustic-style establishment cooks from around the country prepare an amazing assortment of delicious vegetarian dishes, and then add pork to them.

✉ *45 Sv Rojal*
☎ *69 6637*

$ Dining **Budget**

Those looking for a quick drink in a stylish setting could do worse than pop into **Tzabani's** near the northern gates to the Old Town. Here you are guaranteed to get a cool drink, even if you order coffee. A violin–piano duo sets a romantic mood, although several female diners have reported that the fiddle player can get a little 'liberal' with his hands.

✉ *55 Sv Vladko*
☎ *66 3237*

If you fancy a bit of 'club action', why not visit Lublova's hippest adult nightspot, **Ur Verbkriej** ('The Firetrap')? Here you can dance to the latest Euro beats thumping out from the club's 100-watt cassette deck while sipping expensive beers in a sophisticated, smoke-filled atmosphere.

✉ *56 Av Nazjonal*
☎ *63 5437*

Note: Monday is their 'Over 40s' night, referring not to age but the number of weeks since any of the club's patrons have had sex.

HIGHLIGHTS

While the outlying suburbs of Lublova have little to offer in the way of beauty, the **Old Town** remains relatively unscathed by modernisation. This area is closed to all traffic except buses, taxis, motorcycles, cars, bikes and army tanks on military manoeuvres, and a walk round its cobblestone streets is well worth the effort.

Start at the tumbledown **main square** (right), now usually filled with peddlers selling everything from cheap sunglasses to Ukrainian brides. A small lane leading off the main square takes you to the 120m Romanesque tower of the **Gzemgrjo**  **Church**. This would be the oldest standing structure in Lublova, if it were still standing, but unfortunately the upper spire toppled over a few years back when a **satellite TV dish** was ill-advisedly attached. The church itself is often closed, but keys may be obtained from the parish priest, Fr Gromzjot, who can usually be found opposite at the Lublova Toplesh Tavernja.

No visit to this part of Molvania would be complete without popping into the **Old Lublova Gaol** (*Torturak*) on the western outskirts of town. Here you can take a guided tour through one of Medieval Europe's most gruesome places of punishment, where you can see stocks and torture chambers, execution yards and holding cells. The displays are all very realistic due, no doubt, to the fact that the gaol still operates as a **penal facility**. Because of this, visitors should be prepared for a quite thorough strip-search on the way in.

On the outskirts of town is the famous sandstone bluff **Zjkelcziz** where, in 1965, a giant image of former Prime Minister 'Bu-Bu' was carved into the rock. It remains a striking feature, despite the fact that in 1974 portions of the moustache fell off, crushing the visitor's centre below.

Molvanian Moonshine!

The local drink in these parts is *jzornflek*, a fierce liquor usually made from juniper berries and brake fluid. It is traditionally served before funerals (about two weeks before as a general rule, depending on the skill of the intensive care doctor) and it is considered quite an honour to be offered a glass. Rather than cause offence, the polite thing to do is accept a small amount and pretend to drink. If any of the liquor is accidentally swallowed there is no need to induce vomiting. This will happen quite naturally.

For years young lovers visiting Lublova would pay a visit to the ornate **Aquatz Jcejlezic** [right] off Sv. Frortunju where they would make a wish before tossing in a coin. Whilst this magnificent fountain, built in 1465, still exists, the practice of throwing money has sadly been banned after well **organised gangs** of gypsies, many equipped with scuba equipment, began raiding the facility.

Bird on the Wing...

Ornithologists come from all over the world to catch a glimpse of the Molvanian thrush, a small, dun-coloured bird unique to this region. Whilst nothing special to look at, the Molvanian thrush is famous in bird-watching circles for making the shortest migratory journey ever recorded. Each October these birds take off from their nesting grounds 50km south of Lublova and travel 2.5km east. Remarkably, this epic voyage can take some of them anything up to a year to complete and many thousands fly off course or collapse exhausted, far short of their destination.

Opposite the town hall is an interesting art gallery, the **Studja**, specializing in both classic and modern works. A permanent exhibit of paintings by local pseudo-realist Bvorj Gcecvej is permanently closed.

Paws for Thought!

Apart from being a bustling modern metropolis Lublova also happens to be the birthplace of the country's national dog, the Molvanian mastiff. According to the official breed standard:

'... the Molvanian mastiff should have short, stumpy legs (usually three, sometimes four), a wiry grey coat and noticeably undershot jaw. Typically the dog displays a disloyal temperament and is prone to bouts of unprovoked aggression. As a consequence, the animal must be on a muzzle in public. The same rule applies to its owners. Show dogs usually have their ears cropped and most breeders also lop off the tail as it is considered a delicacy. Interestingly, the Molvanian mastiff is the only member of the canine family incapable of licking its own genitals'. from *Dogs of the World* (Universal Press, 1987)

FURTHER AFIELD...

The countryside surrounding Lublova is flat and windswept, dotted with phosphate mines and large salt flats. It is generally regarded as east Molvania's most scenic landscape. Some of the sights worth seeing are listed below.

Monj Vedjev (Mount Vedjev) is a favourite day trip destination for locals and its 178m peak offers both splendid views and hypothermia. To reach the summit, take a bus to the foot of the mountain where you board a **chairlift**. Various signs warn travellers to make sure they have a valid return ticket before getting on the chairlift – not an easy task as these tickets can only be purchased from the vending booth at the top of the mountain. It's also advisable to carry a warm jacket and some emergency flares.

A half-hour drive east of Lublova is stately **Czelm Park**, a lush oasis on the otherwise **barren plain**. Situated in the park is the summer residence of Molvania's most famous modern sculptor **Hzmach Mevtrajo**. This grand chateau and all of its surrounding bronzed statues were donated by Mevtrajo to the public in 1985. In 1986 the public gave them back and the reclusive artist has lived here in miffed silence ever since. An **extensive gallery** operates inside the chateau and entrance is free, although there is a small charge not to have your car vandalised.

A little further on past Czelm Park you'll find a series of **limestone caves**, said by locals to be the home of a fierce dragon (the terrifying *Splidfrik*)! According to folk legend this dragon emerges on nights of a full moon and creeps into town where he selects one unlucky boy or girl who is carried back to the creature's lair and slowly burnt alive. For centuries this delightful tale has been told to Molvanian children as a bed-time story, which may explain the country's unusually high rates of bed-wetting and related sleep disorders.

Visitors to the east of Molvania will be offered a glass of locally brewed zeerstum *(garlic brandy). On no account should it be drunk.*

LAKE SKROTUL

As the swimming and boating centre of eastern Molvania, Lake Skrotul draws thousands of holiday-makers every season. The lake, like much of the region's charm, is artificial and was formed in 1953 when plans to dredge the mighty **River Vzorjmec** went spectacularly wrong and a dam wall was inadvertently created. Sadly, drought – coupled with increased irrigation demands from local farmers – has seen water levels drop alarmingly in recent years, so much so that the 'Lakeside Camping Park' is technically now 3km from the water's edge. Despite this there is still much to see and enjoy at this popular, **semi-aquatic** destination.

Sun-lovers enjoy a summer's afternoon on the shores of Lake Skrotul.

WHERE TO STAY

Apart from the above-mentioned **Camping Park**, it is possible to rent houseboats on the lake. Many of these are diesel powered, others require peddling. Enquiries: Skrotul Ahoyz (☏07/521776870).

WHERE TO EAT

Fresh fish is obviously the food of choice in this part of the world and the shores of Lake Skrotul are lined with cafes and restaurants offering various 'catch of the day' options. The largest and most popular local eatery would have to be **Hzerjman's** (☏92 1768), situated on the main pier. Here diners can select their meal from a large tank near the door, which is great for fish lovers but not so good if you're planning to have steak.

HIGHLIGHTS

The **beaches** surrounding Lake Skrotul are spotless – certainly devoid of sand – and are popular with sun lovers, many of whom reserve their place each morning with a towel or deck chair. So fierce is competition for prime beach space that there have been several reports of towels being booby-trapped by zealous holiday-makers in order to prevent anyone taking their spot – so care should be taken. The waters of Lake Skrotul are surprisingly warm due, in part, to its use as a cooling pond for a nearby coal generator. For those who prefer to stay dry, **cow rides** around the lake are available. Most start from the **cattle sale yards** and finish a few kilometres north at the **Lakeside Abattoirs**.

DZREBO

Some 70km east of Lake Skrotul you'll find the old mining town of Dzrebo. It was here during the Middle Ages that silver was discovered and, had deposits of this precious metal held out for just a few more decades, the townspeople claim Dzrebo could well have become a great European city. As it is, the town is now a great European truck-stop on the **Lutenblag–Lublova Highway**.

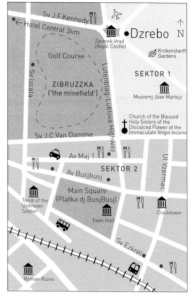

Dzrebo itself is divided into three traditional hamlets, known as Sektor 1, Sektor 2 and Zibruzzka ('the Minefield').

Sadly, there is high unemployment throughout Dzrebo, which has resulted in an underclass of **beggars**, many of whom stand on street corners accosting passers-by. These destitute souls may appear to be down-and-out, but when it comes to seeking donations they are actually quite organized, so much so that many of them even offer **credit card facilities**.

HISTORY

Dzrebo was first discovered in AD 6 by the Roman centurion Callus who, while leading an expedition through the region, became bogged on the flat, swampy plains. After several fruitless weeks attempting to extricate himself from the mosquito-plagued, leech-infested, **stagnant wetlands**, Callus is said to have declared 'this would make an ideal place for a village'. Whilst historians have subsequently conjectured that he may have been speaking sarcastically, his comments were soon acted upon and a small town sprang up. During the Middle Ages the discovery of silver* led to a minor boom that saw much of the city's great monasteries and cathedrals constructed, making Dzrebo a great centre of **Catholicism** throughout the east. When the silver mines finally closed during the 16th century most of the town turned to **prostitution**, but this failed to fully arrest Dzrebo's economic decline. In 1978 the municipality was officially recognized as the flattest city in Molvania.

---

* Locals proudly insist that the 30 pieces of silver given to Judas actually came from Dzrebo. This biblical link is celebrated each year on 25 April (St Traitor's Day).

SHOPPING

Dzrebo is well known for its folk-art products, many of which are sold at **roadside stands**. Amongst the most popular items are corn-husk figures, hand-woven woollen mats and elaborately decorated, wooden marital aids. One word of warning – quarantine laws in several countries prohibit the importation of any articles manufactured from Molvanian agricultural products due to the possibility they may be infested with the rare **bvorvil** mite. If in doubt, declare your purchase to customs officials so that it can be doused in **fungicide**, sprayed with insecticide and then burnt.

HOW TO GET THERE

There is no train or regular bus service to this eastern outpost so for many visitors a car is the only option. However, finding a rental firm willing to let you take a vehicle into the city can be difficult as most have **exclusion policies** that prohibit driving off-road or into Dzrebo. The main concern, of course is theft, and numerous visitors have reported leaving their car for just a few minutes only to have thieves make off with the contents, engine parts or – quite often – the entire automobile. Most locals avoid such incidents by parking in a **guarded garage**, but if this is not an option then the most sensible thing to do is always leave at least one infant in the back seat, preferably crying or with a visibly soiled nappy. Another good deterrent is a steering wheel lock, which can be used to beat would-be thieves over the head.

HOW TO GET AROUND

Buses run frequently and can be hailed by simply waving your hand or, during peak periods, a **small hand gun**. A trip costs $40 and tickets may be purchased from kiosks or the drivers themselves. Remember to cancel one ticket in the machine on the bus for each section travelled, plus an extra one for each zone. Any remaining tickets may be then re-validated using a machine, provided it is not the same machine as originally used.

Dzrebo offers a delightful blend of Renaissance charm and Balkan sleaze.

WHERE TO STAY

The truth is, Dzrebo is not a particularly tourist-oriented town and this fact is reflected in its basic lack of accommodation options. So chronic is the problem that in a recent Molvanian Tourism Board promotion the city's '**Best Boutique Hotel**' award went to a Salvation Army shelter. A better plan for visitors to Dzrebo is to consider staying outside the city in one of the region's many *aggro-turizm* centres where you get to lodge on a **genuine farm** with a local family. Full board and meals are included in the price along with activities such as helping to round up the sheep, helping to chop firewood, helping to slaughter pigs and just generally helping.

$$$ Accommodation Luxury

Claimed to be the first hotel ever to open in Dzrebo, **Jorkjem Palatz** is a beautifully restored chateau right in the heart of the Old Town district. Rooms here are not exactly cheap, but a full Molvanian breakfast (cereal, toast, eggs, sausage and vodka) is included in the price. The hotel also features one of the oldest working elevators in Europe.

✉ 132 Sv Ezkrel
☎ 67 3143
🖷 67 3144
@ jorkjem@molnet.co.mv
🛏 50 🍴 ✐
🖃 DC, MC, V

A little out of town you'll find **Hotjl Golf**. As its name implies this establishment offers not only accommodation but also its own 17-hole golf course. Designed by Molvania's only professional golfer, **Vcez Brailja**, this well maintained course offers challenging bunkers and numerous water bio-hazards that all make for a testing round of golf. (Visitors should note that the course's kerosene-powered golf carts have recently been banned after starting several grass fires.)

✉ 45 Sv J.C. Van Damm
☎ 67 7262
🖷 67 7266
@ golf@molnet.co.mv
🛏 30 🍴 ✐
🖃 DC, MC, V

Note: The hotel itself is clean and modern and, while few of the reception staff speak English, they do respond to basic swear words and obscenities.

Philippe writes...
❝ You've got to laugh at the sight of tourists shacked up in over-priced, sterile, western-style hotels. If you really want to experience the true Molvania you should be homeless. I once spent two weeks on a park bench in Dzrebo covered in cardboard. It's a holiday I'll never forget. ❞
P.M.

$$ Accommodation **Mid-Range**

A good mid-priced accommodation option can be found in the New Town area at **Sjavtzas**. The rooms here are plain and simple with no real surprises apart from the odd frog in the bidet (the owner tells us they're edible!), and there's a pleasant courtyard out the back where guests can hang washing or themselves, depending on their mood.

✉ *48 Av Maj 1*
☎ *62 0690*
@ *sjavtz@molnet.co.mv*
🗝 *19*
▤ *MC, V*

Just across from the taxi stand you'll find **Pensjon Krovoz**, which offers good basic accommodation at value-for-money prices. The place has a relaxed, casual feel and you could almost believe you are staying in someone's home. In fact, you are, and it's not unusual for the owner's children to wander in during the night looking for lost toys or to use their toilet.

✉ *98 Av Busjbusj*
☎ *61 7465*
🗝 *4*
▤ *DC, MC*

$ Accommodation **Budget**

Despite its name, **Hotjl Central** is actually located on the far outskirts of town and takes 45 minutes to reach by public transport. The rooms towards the back are quieter, due to the fact that many of them are underground.

✉ *9 Sv Pudjink*
☎ *66 1212*
@ *cent@molnet.co.mv*
🗝 *72* ▤ *DC, MC, V*

The somewhat seedy **Gronz Mecj**, opposite Dzrebo's main railway station, is popular with businessmen and lone travellers, drawn by the hotel's range of in-room, adult videos available on a pay-for-view basis. Guests accessing this service are assured that the title of the movie will not appear on their bill.

✉ *163 Ul Vzermac*
☎ *65 8673*
🗝 *12*

Note: They will, however, set off a siren and powerful flashing light outside their hotel room door.

Many hotels in Dzrebo offer quality childcare facilities.

> ### We Were Wrong!
> In our last edition it was written that guests staying at the Dzrebo Youth Hostel would find a 'towel' included in each dormitory. This was a typographical error and should, in fact, have read 'trowel' – a reference to the establishment's outdoor toilet facilities.

WHERE TO EAT

Shared tables are a common feature of Dzrebo dining and it's not unusual for couples enjoying a romantic meal out to find themselves joined by a large party of boisterous and often drunk locals. This is considered quite an honour and to complain could cause offence, if not severe **personal injury**. One other point worth remembering – vegetarian meals are hard to find in Dzrebo and dishes described as 'meat free' may legally contain up to 23% pork.

$$$ Dining **Luxury**

The most popular restaurant in Dzrebo is **Hzorvja's**, which specializes in wild game. During the hunting season diners can expect to be served anything from roast boar to oven-baked duck.

   ✉ *37 Av Busjbusj*
   ☎ *66 1972*
   ▭ *DC, MC, V*

Note: Out of season you may have to settle for fresh road-kill.

Another highly recommended eatery is **Pjokotaz**, a centrally-located restaurant popular with business-men and government officials. In addition to hearty stews you'll often be served a side dish of hearty *tsalusky* noodles, which are similar to Italian 'gnocchi' or German 'spaetzle' except for the fact they're hallucinogenic.

   ✉ *67 Av Maj 1*
   ☎ *63 0170*
   ▭ *DC, MC, V*

$$ Dining **Mid-Range**

Located just off the highway, **Vjoy Zjoy** is a trendy bistro offering light vegetarian meals in a relaxed smoke-free environment. It opened in June 2001, but closed within weeks due to lack of customers and has now re-opened as a hamburger shop.

   ✉ *86 Sv J.F.Kennedy*
   ☎ *61 6079*

It seems Chinese cuisine has infiltrated every city in the world and Dzrebo is no exception, with the **Golden Dragon** providing an interesting mix of 'Molvanian-meets-Asian' dishes (even its management structure follows these lines – 'triad-meets-mafia'). Favourites include fried rice with gherkin, sour and sour pork, and the restaurant's signature dish, Peking sparrow.

   ✉ *102 Sv Ezkrel*
   ☎ *67 0898*

Note: All meals are served with rice and MSG.

$ Dining **Budget**

Those after a hearty meal at modest prices could do worse than book a table at **Horgastz Vengelko**, a simple, ground floor cafe just off busy Sv. Izcata. Enticing main courses include roast goose with morello cherries, haunch of wild boar and steak served Molvanian style (i.e. burnt to a crisp). Vegetarians or those on a kosher diet might try the *vecbek*, a pork crepe in which the chunks of meat are cleverly disguised by a thick cheese sauce.

✉ *65 Av Maj 1*
☎ *63 4209*

A Dzrebo farmer prepares his harvest of chestnuts for market. The nuts will be roasted and sold in local restaurants. The farmer will be admitted to hospital with a hernia.

Strictly for the Birds!
After a hard day sight-seeing many visitors like to relax with a coffee and slice of *muczecl* cheese at one of the many outdoor cafes lining Dzrebo main square. One word of warning: the pigeons here are not only voracious, they're one of the few varieties in the world to actually have teeth. Your best bet is to refrain from feeding these disease-ridden scavengers and, if necessary, shoo them away with a rolled-up menu or umbrella. A similar approach works well with the square's numerous buskers and gypsy beggars.

We Were Wrong! Apologies are owed to the owners of the **Zzardmac Bistroj** opposite the old Town Hall. In our last edition this establishment was described as a 'spotless, family-friendly cafe'. This was a typographical error and should have read 'topless family-friendly cafe'. We regret any loss of trade this may have caused to Mr and Mrs Zzardmac and their seven daughters.

HIGHLIGHTS

The **Kastl Rojal** (Royal Castle) dates from the 12th century when Sigmisoid VI ('the Gout Prince') had it built as a summer residence. Tours of this impressive Romanesque edifice are run daily (provided the day is Wednesday) with most visitors keen to see the famous **Royal Treasury** on the ground floor. The main attraction here is, of course, the **Molvanian Crown Jewels** and, despite the collection having been somewhat depleted over the years by Turkish raiders, Nazi troops and unscrupulous cleaning staff, there is still much to see. One of the most fascinating items on display is the *zmittenblag*, a fearsome, jagged sword used by palace officials from the early 14th century onwards for performing circumcisions and trimming hedges.

Dzrebo's largest and most beautiful **park** (the *Villj Krokenstanf*) covers just over 10 hectares on the eastern side of town. A pleasant trail that winds its way through the grassland and over footbridges starts near the main entrance and is a good way to explore the grounds. Numerous signs remind visitors that dogs, bicycles, roller-blades, joggers and prams are all banned. You may, however, lawfully discharge a **firearm** on any day other than Good Friday.

Movie buffs should consider planning a visit to Dzrebo in September to coincide with the city's famous **International Film Festival**, during which budding directors from around the world are invited to submit their work. Last year only two entries were received; both tied for fifth place.

Kaca Jzan Martejz is the house where the 19th century painter Jzan Martejz was born and died, which could perhaps explain the smell. It now serves as a museum for his work.

Eureka!

Nobel Prize near-winner, Willjm Krejkzbec (1891–1943), is without doubt one of Molvania's most famous sons. Krejkzbec was a Dzrebo-born physicist who in 1908 created enormous excitement when he managed to pass an electrical current through a copper plate suspended in chloric acid. Sadly, this ground-breaking achievement proved to have no practical applications, but it still led to a Nobel Prize nomination for the determined pioneer. Of course, Willjm Krejkzbec's academic fame has been largely overshadowed by his much-publicized interest in sado-masochism (see 'Museums' section p106).

The Church of the Blessed Holy Sisters of the Discalced Flower of the Immaculate Virgin Incarnate is a pretty Baroque chapel, which can be a little hard to find as all signs bearing its name have long ago collapsed under the weight of their own letters. In a separate room attached to the back of the church is a large Gothic fresco depicting semi-naked sinners writhing in a pit of flames. It was originally thought by art historians to be a Caravaggio but, upon further examination, turned out to be an advertisement for a local discotheque.

Heaven Scent!
Many visitors to Dzrebo will be interested in taking a tour of the large Vcekjben-Dyir **cosmetics factory** in the city's south-east. 'V-D', as this company is commonly known, makes a wide range of perfumes, deodorants and industrial-strength depilatory creams that are sold throughout Molvania. The Dzrebo-based pharmaceutical giant proudly boasts that none of its products have been tested on animals; however, recent allegations regarding the involvement of gypsy labourers in the 'research and development' phase of production have largely gone unanswered.

Another Dzrebo landmark, the city's famous **mechanical clock** (right), was built in 1746 and every hour visitors would gather below to watch as its mechanical figures would appear and 'dance' to announce the time. These popular shows ended abruptly in 1993 when the scythe belonging to **Father Time** became jammed in Mother Nature's bodice, sparking an electrical fire that fused the two figurines in a pose deemed unsuitable for children.

The changing of the guard ceremony remains a moving spectacle despite budgetry cut-backs forcing many soldiers to march in streetwear.

No visit to Dzrebo would be complete without a stop at the **Tomb of the Unknown Soldier**. Built as a memorial after World War I, the tomb contains the body of a Molvanian soldier shot whilst deserting the front line. Each Sunday at noon there is a ceremonial **changing of the guard** during which the officers on duty will goose-step out of view, change clothes and then shave before returning to stand guard. Above the tomb, flanked by Molvania's national flags, an eternal flame burns (Tues–Sat).

Lake Vjaza

Czarbuncle Mts

WESTERN
PLATEAU

River Uze

oSasava

•Sjerezo

THE WESTERN PLATEAU

[Vesternplat]

THE REGION

Tourists tend to be a little wary of western Molvania, perceiving it as little more than an arc of polluted factory towns full of **high-rise tenement housing** and even higher crime rates. They are, of course, right. But the west of Molvania is also something of a paradox: much of it was despoiled by 40 years of rampant **post-war industrialization**, but here and there you can still find areas of great natural beauty that were only ruined a few years ago. Certainly, much of the region is windswept, barren, cold, isolated and completely lacking in visual charm, but on the upside, it's relatively untouched by tourism.

The Western Plateau contains one of the world's largest **wetland reserves** covering more than 2000 sq km. These swamps are home to over 300 species of migratory birds, 800 plant families and the Molvanian Boy Scout movement who regularly travel here to test their outdoor skills on some of the lowest lying **camping grounds** in Eastern Europe. The best time to experience the wetlands is late May, right after the mosquitoes have been aerially sprayed and before the leeches are fully active.

Of course, for sheer history it's hard to go past the capital of the west **Sasava**, a city that has often been compared to Paris, not so much for its culture or architecture but the fact it's crowded and covered in dog droppings.

Further south you'll find the bustling metropolis of **Sjerezo**, which celebrates its 700th anniversary in 2005. The slogan for the celebrations is 'Sjerezo – Let's Start Over Again' and a number of events are planned including open-air concerts, fireworks displays and a smallpox eradication program.

In the middle of a massive volcanic plain to the north of the wetlands region you'll find the crystal-clear waters of **Lake Vjaza**. No visit to this scenic waterfront locale is complete without an early morning trip to the bustling fish markets where, every Monday at dawn, local fishermen bring their haul. Why the fish market itself doesn't open until Thursday remains a bureaucratic puzzle, but thanks to **modern refrigeration** much of the catch is still edible.

Outside the cities and lake district the rural landscape of the Western Plateau offers much for the visitor prepared to travel 'off the beaten track'. It is here, in small villages, where tradition lives on, in folk dancing, **colourful pottery** and the highly popular, if somewhat barbaric, spectacle of rat-fighting.

Traveller's Tip
*In the west of Molvania, when visiting someone at home the polite thing to say on entering the house is **Drubzko vlob attrizzo**. When visiting someone's place of work, **Klawzitz vlob attrizo** is used. Both expressions literally mean 'Don't shoot'.*

SASAVA

Once a sleepy farming village, the modern city of Sasava has little to show for its agricultural roots apart from a large knackery and **tallow plant** still operating on the northern outskirts. These days Sasava is an industrial and manufacturing centre, producing 30% of the country's automotive equipment and generating 73% of its greenhouse gas emissions. Other exports include locally produced **handicrafts** and human body parts.

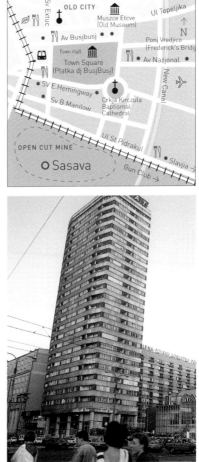

The city may be divided roughly into three areas, each of which can comfortably be covered on foot except for the third, which is an **open-cut mine**. Without doubt the most picturesque section is the Old City, with its winding **cobblestone streets** and quaint, crumbling villas, many dating back to the 1980s. This part of town is closed to private cars but the bumper-to-bumper queues of tour buses, tractors, commercial vans and articulated lorries more than fill the gap.

Sasava residents are known for their hospitality and love talking to foreigners, although their unusual **local dialect** can be a challenge, even for those fluent in Molvanian. It is extremely guttural and features one of the most heavily aspirated 'h's' in linguistic history. Add to this, strange syntactical variations that

A marvel of modern architecture, the Leaning Tower of Sasava was built entirely without foundations. Scientists estimate the structure leans an extra centimetre to the right every time someone slams the lobby door.

mean simple expressions like *en vzec e drivc* ('good luck') are rendered by Sasavans as *vcerc ze ir czejew* ('may your children be fat until their death'). That said, don't be afraid to interact with the locals as you can convey a lot of information with a smile, a nod or a wallet full of *strubls*.

HISTORY

Sasava has suffered many ravages in the course of its long history. It was totally destroyed by the Mongols in 1241 and nearly destroyed again by Slovakian soccer fans during the 1995 **Euro-Balk Championship**. Much of its wealth has come from gold mining and evidence of this heritage can be seen in the **ornate architecture** and opulent interiors of most people's mouths. A few mines continue to operate, including the massive **Tzdorvel pit** on the city's southern outskirts. Tzdorvel made headlines around the world a few years back when a group of miners was trapped, along with several hundred kilograms of gold, deep beneath the ground. The Molvanian Government launched an immediate **inquiry** that concluded a few weeks later that they would have been better off launching an immediate rescue effort. This rescue effort (later the subject of a TV mini-series) was then successfully mounted and the gold was safely brought to the surface. Unfortunately, the miners died.

It's 1947, and one of Sasava's most famous innovators, B.V. Gyzcezcbi, demonstrates his latest invention, the ashtray.

Capital Idea, Bu-Bu!

As the proud residents of Sasava will tell you, for a short period this city occupied a central place in Molvanian political life. The year was 1931 and Prime Minister Busjbusj – ever the statesman – decided to shift the capital from Lutenblag to Sasava in order to establish greater control over the provinces and allow him to be closer to his mother.

Bu-Bu's mother, Sterna Busjbusj.

HOW TO GET THERE

Most people get to Sasava by train or by accident. There is also a **private bus service** from Lutenblag that runs twice-weekly, although one reader advised us that the journey involved numerous unscheduled stops at shops and cafes owned by relatives of the driver. For those preferring to come by plane, there is a busy regional airport in Sasava open to charter flights, but pilots are reminded not to attempt a landing between noon and 2pm as the **control tower** closes for lunch.

HOW TO GET AROUND

Sasava is not an easy city to get around, despite a range of public transport options. The fact is, vandals and hooligans have frightened many commuters away from trains and *trollejbuses*, a trend only partially reversed by the Sasava Transport Police Department's

Sasava's main railway station was deliberately built without a platform in order to give commuters the opportunity to look up each other's dresses.

recently implemented **shoot-to-kill** policy. For the time being it's probably best to steer clear of public transport and take an armoured cab.

On This Day...

In June 1987 Sasava became the first city in Molvania to move its overhead electrical cables underground, a municipal initiative that not only beautified the town but simultaneously eliminated its mole and rabbit population.

Sasava's gold mining heritage is ever present.

WHERE TO STAY

Hotels throughout Sasava are generally clean and smartly furnished with a good range to suit most budgets. Naturally you'll pay more at the top end for extras like air-conditioning or smoke-detectors but most places have **off-season rates** so it's worth asking. Many of Sasava's hotels also offer discounts for seniors, but in the absence of ID you should be prepared for quite a thorough medical examination.

$$$ Accommodation **Luxury**

When the imposing six-storey chateau **Sucjevita** opened in 1996, Sasava did not have a single high-quality hotel. It still does not.

✉ 76 Av Busjbusj
☎ 86 3658
🗝 60 🍴 💳 DC, MC

Comfortable **Cernzy Mejed** is not hard to find. Just head to the main square and look for a palatial red brick villa surrounded by lush gardens; Cernzy Mejed is the concrete apartment block in the laneway directly behind it. The rooms here are basic but clean and the staff all speak English – yet, strangely, appear not to understand it.

✉ 11 Sv B.Manilow
☎ 85 3658
🖶 85 3655
@ mejed@moldi.co.mv
🗝 50 🍴 ✏
💳 DC, MC, V

If it's opulence you're after, book a room at the beautifully restored **Sasava Palatz Hotjl**, right in the heart of the Old City. Suites here are quite palatial and everything is a genuine antique, from the vintage furniture and prints right down to the complimentary chocolate left on your pillow.

✉ 43 Av Busjbusj
☎ 86 2384
🖶 86 2385
@ saspal@moldi.co.mv
🗝 45 🍴 ✏
💳 DC, MC

$$ Accommodation **Mid-Range**

Slavjia is a good mid-range alternative despite the inconvenience of being almost 4km from the city centre. And what you lack in proximity to downtown attractions you more than make up for by being next door to the Sasavan Gun Club's practice facilities. Hotel features include a games room and perhaps the only health club in Europe where pastries are included as part of the work-out program.

✉ 243 Ul St Pidrakul
☎ 82 6947
@ slavjia@molnet.co.mv
🗝 70 ✏
💳 MC, V

Note: Children are welcome but must be kept sedated.

The **Zcejet Kcev**, a Tudor-style chalet that is over a century old, has a comfortable, fresh-air feeling – due in part to the fact a large chunk of its roof is missing. Renovations have been under-way since 2000 and show little sign of ever being completed. The hotel's service can be a little inconsistent – one guest reported a sign on the concierge's desk reading 'back in five days' – but the rooms are cheap and the location central.

✉ *67 Av Nazjonal*
☎ *85 3739*
🖷 *85 3733*
@ *zcejet@moldi.co.mv*
🔑 *16*
🖃 *V*

We Were Wrong!

*In our last edition we mistakenly described the concierge and reception staff at Sasava's **Holidaj Injn** as 'uniformed'. Several guests who sought advice from these people have written to inform us that this description is incorrect. The staff are, by all accounts, 'uninformed'.*

$ Accommodation **Budget**

Claims that Ernest Hemingway once stayed in this modest *pensione* have been questioned by literary historians (it was only built in 1973); however, the **Nyagz Vatj** guesthouse offers good, basic rooms at reasonable prices. The hotel even has its own pool and plans are under-way to have it filled with water in the near future.

✉ *45 SV E.Hemingway*
☎ *89 4664*
@ *ernest@mol.co.mv*
🔑 *21*
🖃 *V*

Hostjl Zipdroff is located on the first floor of a residential apartment building just round the corner from the railway station. This hostel is a good option for those travellers wanting cheap, centrally located accommodation. Upon checking-in each guest gets a locker with a key, large enough for a small suitcase. This is where you sleep.

✉ *125 Av Busjbusj*
☎ *83 3569*
@ *zip@moldi.co.mv*
🔑 *78*
🖃 *DC, MC, V*

Note: There are no shower facilities, but for a small additional cost you will be issued with a packet of moistened towelettes.

For those on a budget, the Art Nouveau **Tjecv Dvor** on the outskirts of Sasava is a good option. The rooms are pretty much what you'd expect, although be warned: the so-called 'Mountain View' suites do not have mountain views (in fact they don't even have windows). The title relates to a faded photograph of the Swiss Alps nailed to one wall.

✉ *Ul St Pidrakul*
☎ *87 5735*
🖷 *87 5734*
@ *dvor@molnet.co.mv*
🔑 *30*
🖃 *V*

WHERE TO EAT

Sasavan cuisine prides itself on local regional flavours, which perhaps explains why so many dishes feature the **pickle**. Freshness is also highly prized and with the Mediterranean a mere two-day drive away you can count on well-frozen seafood. Complement your meal with a bottle of good Sasavan wine, famed for what oenologists call '**volatility**' and chemists call '**combustibility**'. Sasava also boasts numerous mouth-watering *pzotjicas* (cake shops) where you can pop by for a coffee and a slice of *gbebzeci*, a layered cake containing curd cheese, walnuts, cream, chocolate, butter, poppy seeds and eggs. For the weight-conscious there is a '**low-fat**' version that omits the poppy seeds.

The Local Drop...

No-one spends much time in Sasava without being offered a glass of *biljgum*, the locally brewed brandy. This highly scented, thick liqueur is quite unlike anything you've ever tasted – unless you've inadvertently swallowed fabric conditioner – and is generally offered at the end of a meal as a means of prompting guests to leave.

$$$ Dining **Luxury**

To best sample the local cuisine try **Tukzcovo**, a famous *tavernja* in downtown Sasava. Typical dishes here are *kvzerice* (black pudding) and *pvorka* (pork) as well as the house speciality *bzejewc*, which is a peppery stew made from horse meat. Some visitors may find the thought of this last dish distasteful. But it's worth remembering that for your average Molvanian horse, being slaughtered then ground into mince often constitutes a significant lifestyle improvement.

✉ *12 Av Nazjonal*
☎ *84 4765*
▤ *DC, MC, V*

The **Rjidak Kova** is something of a Sasavan landmark, being located 93m up in the city's new TV tower. It's quite expensive, as one would expect from the location, but the food and service are good.

✉ *84 Av Nazjonal*
☎ *86 6265*
▤ *MC, V*

Note: One word of warning for anyone prone to vertigo – Rjidak Kova does have a tendency to sway during high winds or when anyone flushes the lavatory.

$$ Dining **Mid-Range**

Another Sasavan culinary institution is **Tzoyczec**, a large, casual restaurant opposite the train station. In summer you can sit in the garden and order roast suckling pig or lamb. Of course, you're unlikely to get it, as the place only does buttered rolls. It can get a little busy on weekends but prices are good and the serves, like most of the waitresses, are large.

✉ *54 Sv Extuc*
☎ *84 4265*
🖋

A little further out of town you'll find **Zivjukrek**, a delightful modern bistro catering for the tourist trade. It's stylish and elegant with unobtrusive piano music, although the violin player could do with a tuning fork, and the service can be erratic. There is an outdoor terrace for **alfresco dining**; however, the location of the tables – beneath a freeway overpass – does tend to make conversation a little difficult.

✉ *141 Ul St Pidrakul*
☎ *89 0606*
🖋

Svateho is a trendy eatery catering to the coffee-and-cigarette crowd in search of a light meal. Choose from a menu of smoked pastries, smoked sandwiches and smoked, smoked salmon as well as some local specialties such as *hvarus mecac* (sheeps' scrotum and rice).

✉ *35 Av Busjbusj*
☎ *80 4475*

Note: It's worth coming to the 'Svat' on the first Tuesday of each month when the fresh salad bar is re-stocked.

$ Dining **Budget**

For night-owls Sasava is also full of bistros and *tavernjas* where you can drop by for a drink and a chat with the locals. One such *tavernja* is **Fzovrezec Steak Cave** which, whilst not actually in a cave, is cold, damp and dimly-lit. If you just want a light snack and a drink you may stand up at the bar, although by 9pm very few of Fzovrezec's regular patrons are capable of this feat. On weekends patrons have the opportunity of hearing local musicians play the *zamfir*, described by one visitor as a cross between a gypsy violin and a rusty car door.

✉ *6 Sv B.Manilow*
☎ *82 0024*

We Were Wrong!
We have recently been informed that our previous edition's advice about belching loudly and breaking wind at the end of a meal in western Molvania as a means of showing appreciation is apparently not accurate. The contributor responsible has been sacked.

HIGHLIGHTS – IN TOWN

The Old City of Sasava is not large and if you get an early start you can complete a leisurely walking tour of all its highlights in a day, allowing plenty of time for meals and getting mugged.

Note that beggars are a major problem in the city and as a rule they should be avoided; many of their **skin diseases** are exacerbated for the benefit of gullible tourists and handing over money only encourages them to lose further limbs.

From the centre of town take a 10-minute stroll to the **Muszm Antjkq** ('Old Museum'). Follow the Sv. Etxuc past the gardens and turn left at the **cathedral**. Inside the museum you will find a wide range of exhibits including an agricultural display featuring advances in Sasavan **slaughtering techniques** over the years. Admission is free, but there is a small charge for leaving.

The **Badjazcev** is a large villa built as a holiday residence for one of Sasava's wealthiest families, the **Czroyjes**, who made their fortune in gold. A more recent move into Internet publishing saw much of this wealth eroded and the now crumbling facade and cracked roof of this massive residence clearly hints at better times long past. Further concerns over rising damp and asbestos forced the Czroyjes family to finally abandon Badjazcev as a residence in 2001 and it is now used as an old-age accommodation facility.

The **Crkja Kirczula** is a beautifully preserved baptismal chapel of great architectural significance. A cross-shaped baptismal font stands in the centre decorated with a bronze figure of **John the Baptist**, the only known representation of this holy figure trimming his beard.

A typical Sasavan building, featuring its distinctive brown brick and bullet-hole facade.

The **Ponj Vredjico** (Frederick's Bridge) spans the old canal above Sasava and was designed in 1895 by **Grior Bzeulka**, a brilliant Czech architect who came to the attention of city officials when he pioneered a new and far cheaper style of construction that did away with massive buttresses in favour of a delicate interlocking **lattice structure**. By having city officials send him traffic numbers he was able to carefully calculate the maximum weight of vehicle, foot and livestock traffic and arrive at a version that used half the materials of conventional designs. Unfortunately, he failed to account for the average weight of Molvanian women and the bridge collapsed soon

The picturesque Ponj Vredjico.

after completion when two milk maids attempted to cross. The Ponj Vredjico has subsequently been re-built but it is closed to all vehicular traffic and pedestrians over the age of 12.

Directly opposite the chapel is a beautiful **Baroque** villa surrounded by imposing stone walls dating from the 13th century. It's actually a convent, run by Molvania's own **Little Sisters of the Poor**, as you will see from the sign on the gate reading *Zzermcej Ur Barjez* ('Beggars Will Be Prosecuted').

A Tale of Two Bears...

The woods surrounding Sasava are one of the last places in the country where visitors might expect to catch a glimpse of the Molvanian brown bear. One of the friendliest bears in the world, and highly sought-after by shooters, these gentle giants have been hunted almost to extinction. Recently the government introduced a 'closed season', making it illegal to shoot any bear on a Sunday, but this has failed to fully redress the problem. Of more hope is a breeding program being run at the Sasava zoo that has already seen several young bears born in captivity. It is hoped that within a few years these beautiful creatures will be old enough to be released back into the wild so that future generations may have the opportunity to shoot them.

HIGHLIGHTS – OUT OF TOWN

For all the attractions of its city, Sasava also provides an ideal gateway to some stunning countryside and a trip out of town is well worth the effort. Just make sure to wear good walking shoes and remember that **ticks** can be quite a problem in outlying areas of Sasava. If a bite becomes infected the sufferer may experience fever, headache, extreme fatigue and neck stiffness, which are – coincidentally – also the symptoms of a night listening to the **Sasava Symphony Orchestra**.

About 30km south of Sasava in the Cherzjov Forest you'll find a magnificent 17th century **hunting lodge**. It was here that members of the Molvanian Royal Family used to holiday and inside there's a large collection of stuffed animals – rather macabre monuments to the **Archduke of Molvania's** obsession with hunting. The lodge is now open to the public who, for a small price, can also stay here and blast away at a range of specially bred animal targets.

Everywhere you travel around the outskirts of Sasava you will see grape vines as this is one of the biggest wine-producing regions in Molvania. The most commonly grown grape variety is the *plavec*, a small dark fruit with **enormous pips** unique to the area. Wine made from these grapes is often used for sacramental purposes and as a major ingredient in poultry food pellets. Those interested in tasting a glass or two may do so at vineyards such as **Tleojczeks**. This is a family-run affair and visitors are welcome to sample their produce at a small cost. The place can get pretty busy on weekends with scores of visitors lined up at the wooden bar, quaffing mouthfuls of wine and then spitting it out into a large, centrally-placed **spittoon**. For those on a tight budget it is possible to wait outside and sample the contents of the spittoon for a slightly **reduced cost**. Bottles can also be purchased, though be aware that *plavec* wine has a slightly higher-than-usual alcohol content (47%) and is best left to breathe after opening, preferably for about six months.

The hills of Cherzjov Forest make an ideal place to enjoy a picnic, undisturbed by large numbers of people or trees.

SJEREZO

Once considered the capital of Molvania's 'wild west', the bustling city of Sjerezo has long since shed its image as a rough, brawling industrial town. No doubt the imposition of martial law in 1998 has helped speed this process up, and these days visitors who make the effort to cross the bleak **tundra** surrounding this western frontier city will find a huge range of attractions to enjoy.

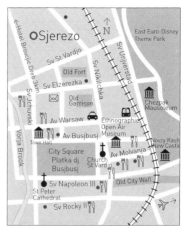

Without doubt the best known of these would have to be the recently re-opened East Euro-Disney Theme Park, which remains a popular drawcard despite negative publicity involving last year's **roller-coaster** derailment and subsequent inferno.

Sjerezo is also famous as permanent host city of the glamorous Miss Molvania beauty pageant in which the country's most **stunning young ladies** parade before the judges on a **specially reinforced stage** in a range of dress categories, including evening gowns, swimwear, peasant costumes and – a recently added category – nurses' uniforms.

Sjerezo's East Euro-Disney Theme Park continues to draw visitors with its high tech rides and cosmopolitan atmosphere.

But for all its modernity, the past is very important to Sjerezo. Nowhere is history better celebrated than at the famous **Ethnographic Open Air Museum**, where the local Historical Re-enactment Society brings to life many of the great battles fought in this city with a real eye to detail that can only come from a combination of authentic uniforms and live ammunition.

Sjerezo's magnificent **Old Town** is among the most extensive in Europe, occupying a total of 240 hectares. Among the highlights is a structure believed to be the oldest working **public lavatory** in Molvania. Built from stone, it was constructed in 1329 – coincidentally the year it was last cleaned.

HISTORY

The village of Sjerezo first came to prominence in the 9th century when the disgraced **Bishop of Lutenblag**, Karzj Wenlecze, was caught in a compromising position with a parishioner's mule and, as punishment, exiled to this western outpost for the term of his unnatural life. Bishop Wenlecze immediately set about attempting to unify and protect the town. Fearing attack from Turkish invaders, he commissioned his best artisans to build a **massive wall** around the entire city, 25m high and 6m thick. This task was soon completed, but for some reason they forgot to put in a **gate** and the residents of Sjerezo were cut off from the rest of Molvania for almost a year before a small entrance (known by locals as the '*katflaap*') could be carved out.

Try This One On For Size!
The father of Molvanian haute couture, Haut Ketur Sr. (1911–1967), was without doubt his country's most distinguished fashion designer. Obsessed with high collars, robust belts and heavy fabrics, he is credited with inventing the straight-jacket.

During the 14th century Sjerezo came to be known as a spa town, with thousands of travellers coming from all over the country to take of its healing waters. These days Sjerezo still boasts some 140 **mineral springs**. Most of these are used for treating diseases of the kidneys and respiratory tracts, although one, currently the subject of scientific investigation, is claimed to increase the size of the male **genitals**. It is currently booked out until the winter of 2012.

The 20th century was a turbulent time for Sjerezo. After World War II its government was faced with massive unemployment, hyper-inflation and growing breadlines. In 1982 a new governor, **Claujz Vernkiz**, (right) was elected as head of the DPP (Democratic People's Party). His first move was to cancel all future elections and declare himself **supreme leader**, a position he has held with often ruthless determination ever since.

Governor Claujz Vernkiz
(Photo courtesy CIA)

Water Watch
Due to several years of below average rainfall the entire city of Sjerezo is in the middle of severe water restrictions. At the time of writing, residents were prohibited between 9am and 5pm from watering their gardens, washing cars or drowning unwanted domestic pets. Even the local police are banned from using water cannons to break up public protest meetings, having to rely instead on tear-gas and rubber bullets.

SHOPPING

Sjerezo is famous for its fashion industry and throughout the Old Town you can visit small, dimly-lit workshops where talented **local tailors** ply their trade. Of course, many visitors are often disturbed by the sight of young children employed in these factories, but bear in mind that Molvanians have a different definition of when a person can legally be classified as an adult. It is generally accepted by most parents that after the age of nine their offspring cease to be a 'child' and officially become an asset.

HOW TO GET THERE

Given the large distances and poor state of the roads, driving to Sjerezo is not generally advisable unless you have rally car racing experience and a working GPS. Many visitors choose to arrive by plane and there is a regular service to **Anton Jchuvski Airport** – named after Sjerezo's highly-decorated World War I ace (1897–1922) who single-handedly shot down 18 planes, six of them belonging to the enemy. A reminder for inbound passengers: domestic flights land at Terminal B, international flights at C or E. Transit passengers can take a bus from Terminal A or D, depending on where their flight originated from. Terminal B is reserved for those travelling with **livestock**.

HOW TO GET AROUND

Sjerezo has a well-developed transport system involving trams, *trollejbuses*, trains and light rail. Due to a bureaucratic oversight, however, these various modes of public transport all cover the same short section of road, leaving most other parts of the city largely unserviced.

Trams are probably your best bet for getting around and **tickets** can be bought on board from the *konduktor* who, incidentally, is also authorized to sign **statutory declarations** and officiate at weddings. The best way to see the Old Town is on foot, preferably your own, although there are beggars based at the railway station who offer a **piggyback service**. This is a charming local custom and the stamina of these emaciated vagrants is nothing short of amazing.

A cyclist enjoys a pleasant afternoon ride along Sjerezo's de-militarized zone.

WHERE TO STAY

Despite being a little off the regular tourist track, Sjerezo still has plenty to offer in the way of accommodation. In the heart of the **Old Town** you'll find luxurious, if somewhat faded, establishments dating back to by-gone centuries, whilst the surrounding suburbs have plenty of cheap, clean, comfortable hotels provided you're not looking for all three at once. Meanwhile, in outlying rural areas you can spend the night in rustic farm-style lodgings that completely belie their origins as decommissioned **Soviet gulags**. Guests staying in the centre of Sjerezo's Old Town should be aware that the area opposite the **Post Office** is a popular hang-out for drug dealers, prostitutes and transsexuals, and is best avoided, or visited, depending on your inclination.

$$$ Accommodation **Luxury**

At the top end it's hard to go past **Vjakm Palatz**, the oldest and most luxurious hotel in Sjerezo. Rooms at the palace are large with sweeping views and private facilities. Some of the suites boast fireplaces and plans are under-way to install chimneys in the near future.

✉ 54 Av Molvanja
☎ 36 5747
🖷 36 5748
@ vjakm@moldi.co.mv
🔑 70 🍴 ✐ ☰ DC, V

Another historic building now serving as a hotel is the **Kostol Vjardi**. The rooms here are spacious with high ceilings and many of the staff are friendly, whilst others speak English but, sadly, not both. One feature of this hotel is that they offer a babysitter service for just ⑤70 per hour.

Note: All their nannies are trained in first aid and hand-to-hand combat.

✉ 36 Av Busjbusj
☎ 34 8484
🖷 34 8485
@ kostol@moldi.co.mv
🔑 70 🍴
☰ DC, MC, V

One final Sjerezo institution – quite literally, as it used to be a psychiatric hospital – is the **Hotjl Lunatik** across from the city square. Extensively renovated in the 1980s this centrally-located establishment even has an underground car park which, during particularly wet winters, doubles as an indoor pool.

Note: The complimentary fruit bowl in each room is purely decorative and should not under any circumstances be eaten.

✉ 12 Av Molvanja
☎ 32 3976
🖷 32 3976
@ jkez@molnet.co.mv
🔑 70 🍴
☰ DC, MC, V

$$ Accommodation **Mid-Range**

Pejzuca is a bright, comfortable hotel located within easy walking distance of the Old Town. The rooms are clean, if a little on the spartan side, and a full breakfast is included in the cost – although it is only served between 5.30am and 6am.

✉ *87 Sv Napoleon III*
☎ *37 0870*
🖷 *37 0871*
@ *pejzuca@molnet.cv*
🛏 *30* 🍴 ≣ *MC, V*

Hotjl Brovcjic Dreb is a drab concrete building some 15km from the city centre, which is at least close to the airport – a fact disturbingly highlighted in November 2001 when a Ukrainian cargo plane on final approach clipped the **penthouse** roof.

✉ *20 Ul Pokzi*
☎ *36 4395*
🖷 *36 4396*
@ *dreb@moldi.co.mv*
🛏 *23* ≣ *DC, MC*

> **We Were Wrong!** In a previous edition Sjerezo's **Hotjl Jakvekz** was mistakenly described in this section as 'appealing'. It is, in fact, 'appalling'.

$ Accommodation **Budget**

Hotjl Vcejlav – formerly the Stock Exchange, and before that a piggery – is a small, family-run inn offering moderate-size rooms at a budget price. Despite the **low rates** all rooms have TV, although the only one that works would appear to be in the manager's office where it is permanently tuned to loud and surprisingly aggressive game shows.

✉ *34 Sv Elzerezka*
☎ *35 5747*
@ *vcejlav@mol.co.mv*
🛏 *12*

A short bus ride east from the city centre will take you to the **Pensjon Prazakuv**. From the outside this unassuming hotel looks like a seedy, dilapidated relic desperately in need of a clean. It is.

✉ *142 Sv Unjverstad*
☎ *30 3974*
@ *praza@molnet.co.mv*
🛏 *4* ≣ *DC, MC*

Health department raids and a spate of fires have somewhat reduced the number of youth hostels still operating in Sjerezo, but one of the oldest can be found a few kilometres west of the city. The **Pensjon Beddbugg** is popular with backpackers and students, and offers large, semi-ventilated dormitories, shared bathrooms and syringe disposal facilities.

✉ *97 Sv Nikitchka*
☎ *31 9023*
🖷 *31 9024*
@ *bugg@molnet.co.mv*
🛏 *90*
≣ *DC, MC*

WHERE TO EAT

For the past decade or so Sjerezo restaurants have developed something of a reputation as tourist traps where unsuspecting visitors would be presented with all sorts of **hidden charges** and fees at the end of a meal. Fortunately, the most seriously unscrupulous operators have been forced out of the restaurant trade and into local government. It still pays to carefully check the bill and query items such as *elejtrij chaj* ('15% electric lighting surcharge').

$$$ Dining **Luxury**

The elegant **Fakjrezic** restaurant is regarded as one of Sjerezo's most upmarket eateries, featuring, as it does, linen tablecloths and indoor toilets. Naturally it's popular with diplomats and local politicians who are attracted by the discrete atmosphere and lingerie-clad waitresses.

✉ *34 Av Molvanja*
☎ *39 4023*
▤ *DC, MC, V*

Magzicj is situated atop Sjerezo Hill. A favourite of visiting dignitaries and Russian mafia figures (which in Sjerezo is often the same thing), this classic restaurant offers excellent views of the **Old City** for those lucky enough to have window seats and a set of **binoculars**. The service is good and the menu features a wide range of traditional (deep-fried) and modern (fried) dishes, as well as the usual variety of rich, cream-filled cakes for dessert, all served with seasonal fruit (pan-fried).

✉ *64 Sv Napoleon III*
☎ *33 3856*
▤ *DC, MC, V*

Vorgzjen Marj is a fetching neoclassical building from the 19th century, with dark, high-back benches in the front and cosy elegant sofas and chairs upstairs, making it the perfect place to settle back and enjoy a **sumptuous feast**. Unfortunately, you can't because it's a furniture shop. There is, however, a soup kitchen next door that does a good broth.

✉ *12 Av Molvanja*
☎ *39 4557*

$$ Dining **Mid-Range**

The best way to sample authentic Sjerezo-style cuisine is by visiting a *tavernja* such as the bustling **Mdejazcic**, just off the city's main square. Here you can feast on such local delicacies as *jgormzca* (meat roasted on a spit) and *nzemji* (meat roasted in spit). A **gypsy band** plays each evening from 7pm until whenever local authorities manage to move them on.

✉ *6 Av Molvanja*
☎ *39 2334*

Those seeking a slightly less boisterous dining experience might try U Zlaje Vokjum, a casual lunch and dinner bistro opposite the Town Hall. There's a good range of meat and pasta although one diner advised us that the heavily-battered '**Fisherman's Basket**' is, in fact, just batter cut into the shape of various seafoods.
Note: The basket itself is said to be more edible.

✉ *56 Av Warsaw*
☎ *34 5768*

Varji's is a bright, funky pizza bar offering an interesting range of toppings, such as the 'Anchovy and Fig Supreme', which you can eat in or vomit up at home. There's even a free delivery service to anywhere within 100m of the restaurant.

✉ *62 Sv Rocky II*
☎ *39 4808*

$ Dining **Budget**

The relaxed, friendly bistro **Tbzut** was a favourite of Sjerezo writer and bon vivant Gyorj Vlerbek who ate here regularly until his death in 1996 from salmonella poisoning. Meals are good value with crusty bread and cured meats a specialty.
Note: The summer terrace offers alfresco dining with a difference. It's inside a cellar.

✉ *35 Av Molvanja*
☎ *34 4808*
🖉

Just west of the main square and across the bridge over tiny Vorja Brook, **Erdjesz** is a friendly, light-filled bistro popular with residents and tourists alike. The food is typically Molvanian – heavy, hearty and laden with unidentifiable brown bits.

✉ *32 Sv Jchuvski*
☎ *30 9705*

Vorbcek Vorbcek (literally, 'Healthy Healthy') is an unassuming bistro good for those watching their weight, as the energy required to chew any of their offerings far exceeds the energy provided by the food.

✉ *65 Av Molvanja*
☎ *34 8808*

Bottoms Up!
In Sjerezo, red wine is generally served with most meals (except for breakfast, which is usually accompanied by vodka). The most popular local variety is *Jzankova*, a full-bodied claret with fruity overtones and a slightly acidic finish – so much so it has been known to eat through stainless steel goblets.

HIGHLIGHTS

Like many Molvanian cities, most activity is centred around the **town square**. Sjerezo's historic square was first laid out in the 16th century and, until quite recently, was regularly used for **military parades** and exercises. However, due to its uneven cobblestone surface, marching soldiers would frequently sprain ankles and tear cruciate ligaments – so much so that historians have estimated between 1914 and 1945 Molvania had more troops wounded here than on any **battlefield** in Europe. These days the square is a great place to relax on a summer's day with a warm beer or cold coffee at one of the many **outdoor cafes**. On weekends there's a folk market selling traditional hand-made pirated DVDs.

Sjerezo's town square is no longer used for military parades. It does, however, continue to attract lunatics.

Just off the main square is a delightful little chapel, the **Church of St Vardjo**, where you will find numerous fine examples of Gothic art, including several impressive **bronze panels** depicting important religious events such as the Annunciation, Christ's betrayal in the garden of Gethsemane and Molvania's near victory in a 1994 World Cup qualifier. There are also some excellent works of art inside the **sacristy** adjoining the church, however this building is often closed. One practical tip – try approaching the uniformed guard at the church gates and slip him ₷50. He won't take you anywhere but the naked shots of his wife aren't bad.

The Palace guards of Sjerezo were said to be the personal favourites of King Svardo III under whom they were officially known as the 'Royal Molvanian She-Boys'.

A worker at the Sjerezo nuclear power plant proudly demonstrates the central reactor core, safely protected by her lead-lined shawl.

At the entrance to the Old Town is a massive set of **battlements** built by Sjerezo's Duke Ijodzor the Wise during the 14th century to protect the town from invasion. Some of the **original walls** were up to 6m thick, which would have made them impenetrable, except for the fact they were constructed out of papier mâché. Only a few sections remain standing.

Sjerezo's main **cathedral** is dedicated to St Peter and, unusually, was built not by foreigners but by the town's local Christian population. Records are sketchy but it is believed construction commenced in 1209. Due to ongoing industrial action, including an official 'go-slow' campaign that ran for several decades, by 1314 only half of the foundations were complete and authorities decided to abandon the heavily unionized local workforce in favour of Venetian architect **Giovanni Berninici**. The project still took another 30 years to complete, but by 1344 Sjerezo boasted one of the finest three-walled cathedrals in all of Eastern Europe.

For Art's Sake!

Many visitors will no doubt have heard of the Gyrorik Art Gallery, an institution that made headlines a few years back when its curator Vbrec Mzecjenj suspected a Rembrandt landscape in the gallery's possession may, in fact, have been painted over a rare, and far more valuable, self-portrait of the Dutch master. Under the curator's guidance a painstaking restoration process was commenced in which the outer layer of the painting was delicately stripped away. The work took almost 16 months and eventually revealed nothing underneath. With the original work destroyed, all that remained of value was the frame, which now holds a copy of Mr Mzecjenj's letter of resignation.

The **Novzy Kastl** (New Castle) was constructed between 1564 and 1571. This six-storey Renaissance building was originally used as a **watchtower** and later became the town's live clock, with the time being announced every half-hour by a trumpeter. This tradition continued right through until the 1950s when the last **official time-keeper** was sacked for turning up to work late. It is sometimes possible to climb the castle; the viewing platform on top offers excellent shots of the Old Town for photographers and snipers alike.

Whilst on the subject of climbing, a few kilometres west of Sjerezo is the **old garrison** (*Guardjslaad*), perched dramatically on top of a steep hill overlooking the city. The three hour walk up to the top is well worth the effort, although for those daunted by such an arduous climb there are **donkeys** available for hire at the base of the hill. A return trip will cost you ⑀55, which can be paid directly to the donkey's handler before heading off. A word of warning – some visitors have reported being kicked and even bitten by these ill-tempered beasts and so care should be exercised. Fortunately, the donkeys themselves are quite placid.

No trip to Sjerezo would be complete without a visit to the **grave** of local composer **Vicktor Chezpak** (left). A child prodigy, he could play piano, violin, flute and cello by the age of 10. Mysteriously, this ability largely deserted him a few years later and by the age of 14 all he could manage was a few tunes on the harmonica. Despite such setbacks he continued writing and performing music, including the classic *Yoj Molva!*, a rite-of-passage **anthem** often sung at

Vicktor Chezpak

national gatherings. The massive marble **mausoleum** stands at the end of an avenue of silver birch trees and is unique, as much for its intricate architecture as for the fact that Chezpak is not actually yet dead. According to an inscription on the door the **cenotaph** was simply financed and constructed by local music lovers in anticipation of the long-awaited event.

Anyone approaching Sjerezo by road from the south will notice a large **steel bridge** over the **River Gjorzecer**. A small plaque at one end of this bridge records that it remains the scene of Molvania's worst railway disaster. It was here on a foggy night in 1978 that a passenger service returning from Lutenblag collided with a freight train loaded with iron ore. Both trains then toppled off the bridge and onto a fully loaded pleasure barge making its way up the River Gjorzecer. A subsequent government inquiry cleared both drivers, but did call for an immediate end to production of 'Molvanian Candid Camera'.

LAKE VJAZA

Despite living in a landlocked country, Molvanians love to spend time by the water, and mighty Lake Vjaza provides the perfect destination. Formed in the 1950s, when Soviet nuclear testing inadvertently perforated a massive **artesian bore**, Lake Vjaza now covers some 26 sq km. In its early days the impoundment developed a reputation for being badly polluted after thousands of dead waterbirds and fish were found washed up on the shore but, thanks to a massive **re-stocking program**, Lake Vjaza is now teeming with mutant fish.

Every summer thousands of holiday-makers descend on this inland waterway to spend a few exotic weeks enjoying the many aquatic-based **activities**, such as boating, water-skiing, wind surfing and trolling for carp. During these warmer months visitors can take a **cruise** across the lake on board a colourfully-decorated *pletzna*, an old-fashioned canopied wooden boat similar to a Venetian gondola except for the fact it's shorter and powered by diesel. For a small tip your captain will launch into a **traditional folk-song**. For an additional tip he'll stop.

There are also numerous **sandy beaches** around Lake Vjaza that are ideal for swimming provided care is taken to avoid the water. Naturally enough, the entire area is very popular with **nudists**, and several stretches of shoreline are designated 'clothes free'. Binoculars are available for hire at most nearby shops.

HOW TO GET THERE

Situated in the far north of the Plateau region, Lake Vjaza requires a bit of effort to get there.

For a road crossing a flat plain, the main highway features a surprising number of tight curves and hair-pin bends, a result of having been designed by undergraduate engineering students at **Sasava University**. If you don't have a car, remember that buses leave Lutenblag for Lake Vjaza twice weekly and are towed back at the end of each month.

WHERE TO STAY

Without doubt the largest and most popular place to stay at Lake Vjaza is the youth-oriented **Klub Zzebo** on the shores of a semi-protected but still very windswept southern bay. Despite seeming a little out of place in Central Europe, this **Polynesian-themed** holiday village draws large crowds of young tourists who come to enjoy sun, sand and drinking vodka out of a coconut. It was originally built in the 1980s, and following recent renovations, including, the installation of toilet facilities, continues to be booked out during the summer period. Numerous **activities** are provided free to guests, including wind-surfing, wave-jumping and kite-sailing, or you can just relax and sunbathe behind one of the resort's purpose-built **wind-shelters**. There are also regular free lectures on sexually transmittable diseases.

> *Philippe writes...*
> "*Can you believe it? Thousands of tourists paying big bucks to stay in a tacky lakeside holiday village when, just a few hundred metres away, I found lodging at an authentic 17th century shepherd's cottage. Lying there on my $\eS$50 a night slat-bed I could hear the sound of young backpackers down the road – dancing, drinking, taking drugs and copulating all night long. I knew where I'd rather be!* "   *P.M.*

WHERE TO EAT

Lipza Daz is one of many popular fish restaurants overlooking the magnificent waters of Lake Vjaza. Here diners can choose their meal from any of the creatures washed up on the lake shores.

Another popular backpacker eatery is **Bistroj Vjaza**, located just a short walk from the main jetty. This funky bistro is relaxed, cosy and – as of 2002 – officially asbestos-free.

The traditional dancers of Lake Vjaza not only entertain but will, for a small extra fee, remove head lice.

HIGHLIGHTS

Recent re-stocking programs have seen various species of fish successfully introduced back into the lake. As a consequence, **fishing** has become a very popular activity and most methods are permitted, such as bait and netting. In the interests of conservation there are, however, some restrictions on the use of harpoons and **underwater explosives**.

Just a few kilometres from the lake's main beach you will find one of the largest and most dimly-lit gaming houses in Central Europe, the recently-built **Grandj Vjaza Kasino**. Many visitors have compared this facility to Las Vegas, not so much for its facilities as the fact that both are situated in a desert and lit by neon. Here you can enjoy all the popular staples such as blackjack, roulette and poker, as well as more localized games like *cvardo* (in which players must select a numbered ball between one and 12 and then stuff it down the brassiere of the correspondingly-numbered **pole dancer**). Entrance $80, children free.

During a papal visit to Western Plateau in 1978, John Paul II's 'Pope-Mobile' broke an axle just north of Lake Vjaza. The offending pot-hole is now considered a holy site.

Dive! Dive! Dive!

Often docked at the northern edge of Lake Vjaza is the Molvanian navy's only **submarine**, the *Zcjormst*. Despite the unlikely threat of attack, this Russian-built vessel regularly patrols the waterway. In keeping with official policy the government refuses to confirm or deny whether the *Zcjormst* is equipped with nuclear weaponry but the tendency of its crew to all wear lead-lined uniforms and carry Geiger counters suggests some degree of atomic capability. On most weekends the *Zcjormst* is open to the public, and the crew are more than happy to show visitors around. Naturally enough, certain areas (such as the weapons room) are off-limits, but a small tip will open most doors.

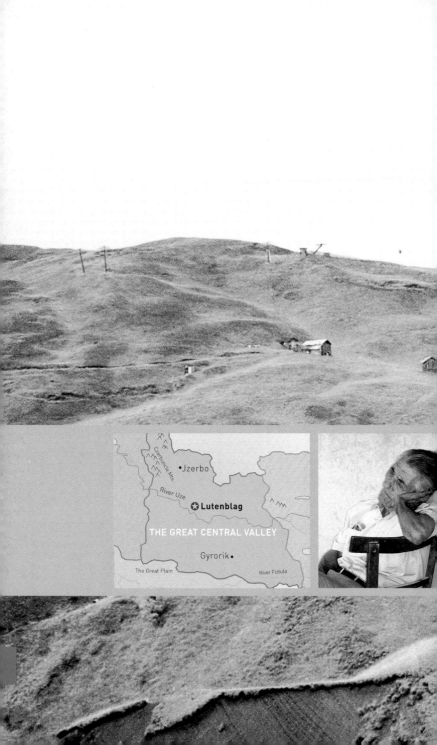

Jzerbo

Carbuncle Mts

River Uze

✪ Lutenblag

THE GREAT CENTRAL VALLEY

Gyrorik

The Great Plain

River Fiztula

THE GREAT CENTRAL VALLEY
[Grandj Kentral Valljk]

THE REGION

Though generally overlooked by tourists, central Molvania is very much the country's heart and soul. This is where the nation was born and where much of its folklore and **deep-rooted traditions** continue to flourish. In many villages here it's not uncommon for elderly women to grab you by the ears and spit three times into your face, said to offer protection from evil spirits. It won't, however, protect you from **tuberculosis**, and appropriate medical precautions should be taken.

The beauty of the Central Valley region lies not so much in its architecture as in its inspiring natural landscapes. The area is home to the eighth-highest **mountain range** in Europe, the impressive **Czarbuncle Mountains**. In winter when the rest of the alps are overrun with hordes of skiers these slopes are generally free of crowds. Unfortunately, due to prevailing dry winds, they're also free of snow for most of the season. Thanks to local ingenuity, however, a **de-commissioned jet engine** combined with a bank of Slurpee machines provides a passable cover of artificial snow.

A local angler prepares to wet a line.

Outdoor activities are widely available in the Central Valley and every year adventure-minded tourists come here to camp, hike, climb and jet boat across one of the many massive sinkholes that dot the limestone plains. Sadly for the adventure tourism trade, at the time of writing the **Vzintga Bungee Jumping Centre** was still closed pending a coronial inquest into the tensile strength of aged rubber – but there is still much here to satisfy the adrenalin junkie. And of course, no visit to the area would be complete without wetting a line in the hope of bagging a trophy-sized *kjark* (see opposite), an elusive fish native to the region. Prospective anglers are, however, reminded of the need to purchase a **fishing licence** (valid for one year) from any post office as well as a fishing permit (valid for a day, week or month), which can be obtained from the **Ministry of Agriculture** office in Jzerbo. This permit must be validated by an authorized Fisheries Inspector both before you commence angling and again each time you land a fish. **Heavy penalties** apply for those caught without the correct forms and foreigners risk having their visas extended.

JZERBO

The unofficial capital of the Great Central Valley region, Jzerbo may not look all that inviting to the first-time visitor, with its jumble of grim Soviet-era block housing and concentration of heavy industry. But thanks to frequent, heavy smog, many of these visual eye-sores remain hidden from the average visitor. There are also several pockets of **historical charm**, including some of the oldest slums in Europe, and after a few days here you can leave behind the trappings of the modern world – pollution, hustle, antibiotics – and step back into a genuine Renaissance-era village.

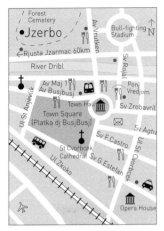

For music lovers, the **Jzerbo Symphony Orchestra** give regular recitals during the summer months, although concert-goers should be warned that due to financial restraints portions of these performances may often be pre-recorded. As a general rule, the strings, woodwind and brass sections are taped, but you can pretty much count on the percussion to be live.

At the other end of the cultural scale, Jzerbo is the centre of Molvania's **fox hunting community**, and visitors to the city's outlying regions might be lucky enough to witness a hunt in full swing. Horses are, of course, involved but, unlike their English counterparts, Molvanian hunters don't use hounds; preferring to track, corner and rip open the throat of their prey themselves. As in England, however, the sport remains controversial with many **animal rights advocates** calling for it to be banned. Whilst this is still several years away, there are moves to phase it out as a school sport.

To Catch a Kjark...

A member of the eel family, the *kjark* is recognized by its dark, slimy scales and pungent smell. Some specimens also have a brown stripe along their flanks, but this is merely a fungal growth. The highly sought-after *kjark* thrives in muddy, polluted conditions, making it ideally suited to the waterways of central Molvania. Despite growing up to 10kg, *kjark* are not highly noted for their fighting qualities, tending to give up immediately after being hooked. Anglers should take care as they have sharp, dagger-like teeth, although in older fish many of these are often missing. The most popular method of angling is to use live bait (generally a frog or newly-born kitten), although in shallow water a small bore rifle can also be useful. Table quality is considered good to fair, with the flesh described as tasting something like juvenile dolphin.

HISTORY

Interestingly, historians are unsure precisely how old the village of Jzerbo actually is. In 1974 a major **archaeological dig** was commenced at the site of its earliest settlement, but this research project had to be called off after residents complained it was interfering with their underground TV cable.

Earliest records date back to the 8th century and indicate that Jzerbo was caught up in numerous battles with invading armies. Years of **constant warfare** in the vicinity of the town led to all buildings being makeshift wooden houses that could easily be burnt as a preliminary **defence** to the city, a practice that perhaps explains the strong tradition of arson that exists amongst the local citizenry today. By the Renaissance, Jzerbo was a very advanced city and in 1681 it published Molvania's first daily newspaper, the *Gzorme-mec*, which was also the first daily paper in Europe to feature lithographs of **semi-clad wenches** on page three.

Sadly, the city was wracked by civil conflict for much of the next century, as various local warlords fought for control. The eventual victor, Duke **Hrojkac III** (Hrojkac the Ruddy), ruled for almost two decades. A despotic autocrat, he crushed all opposition with ruthless tyranny (although he did introduce the **metric system**) until his overthrow in 1796, when the people of Jzerbo rose up under the command of a young, charismatic peasant, **Ljocek Vrutklen** ('the yokel king'). This peasant leader's first move was to call for free and democratic elections, in which he received 123% of the vote, restoring Jzerbo to its position as a peaceful and modern Molvanian city. In 1801 **torture** was abolished as part of the legal process, although it remained popular as a means of **public entertainment** until the 1970s.

Jzerbo is situated on the idyllic River Dribl.

WHEN TO GO

Whilst there are no specific festivals or events scheduled in Jzerbo, one should avoid the conclusion that the residents are either bland or lacking in excitement. As the window of the local **Buro dj Turizm** declares, 'In Jzerbo every day is a holiday!', which could explain why the office seems to be permanently shut.

HOW TO GET THERE

The most common way of reaching Jzerbo is by bus from Lutenblag. The government bus line **AutoMolv** operates a weekly service that generally runs non-stop (it has no brakes), although there are also several private companies. You can also fly **AeroMolv** from Lutenblag, however, the trip often takes several hours as company policy demands pilots keep circling until all on-board alcohol has been purchased and consumed by passengers. Rental cars are not recommended in Jzerbo (it is, after all, the birthplace of road-rage) due to the **narrow streets** and the fact that local residents may legally drive at the age of nine.

HOW TO GET AROUND

For visiting all but the furthest reaches of town, *trollejbuses* are your best bet, though they tend to be uncomfortably crowded throughout most of the day and it is often necessary to jostle with other passengers in order to alight and disembark. During busy **peak periods** a small knife or blood-filled syringe may be useful to clear a path. Remember, **smoking** is permitted only at the back of the bus; the same rule applies to expectoration, although this by-law is not so rigorously enforced.

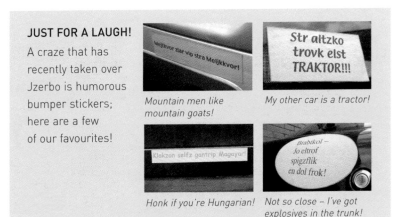

JUST FOR A LAUGH!

A craze that has recently taken over Jzerbo is humorous bumper stickers; here are a few of our favourites!

Mountain men like mountain goats!

My other car is a tractor!

Honk if you're Hungarian!

Not so close – I've got explosives in the trunk!

WHERE TO STAY

The truth is, Jzerbo has struggled to keep up with demand for **quality accommodation**, and visitors to the city may be disappointed by the limited choices available at the top end. Hopefully, this situation will soon be remedied as the local government has been attempting to kick-start hotel development by offering **incentives** to investors in the form of tax relief and immunity from prosecution. There are, however, plenty of mid-range and budget accommodation options to be found within the city. Decent lodging in **outlying areas** is, of course, a little more difficult to come by and there are very few 'hotels' as such, although several farming communities offer limited **shed-and-breakfast** accommodation.

$$$ Accommodation **Luxury**   Not Applicable.

$$ Accommodation **Mid-Range**

The location of the modern accommodation complex **Hotjl Kentral** is not great: the middle of a dreary housing estate about 5km from the town centre. However, the hotel does have its own extensive private grounds where guests can enjoy a fair degree of tranquillity surrounded by mature trees and razor wire fencing. Guests come back to the Kentral year after year, not only for the attentive service but, to search for loved ones believed buried in the hotel grounds.

✉ 296 Sv G.Estefan
☎ 41 9206
🖷 41 9207
@ kentral@moldi.co.mv
🛏 106 🍽
▭ DC, MC, V

Plavniekji is a medium-sized establishment just to the north of Jzerbo's city centre with plenty of small, well-kept rooms. Naturally, prices are higher during the summer months when cleaning staff arrive, but even then you can get a double room for under $100.

Note: This tariff includes a breakfast that is adequate but not generous and guests are reminded that severe penalties apply to anyone attempting to help themselves to an extra slice of toast.

✉ 12 Av Vrutken
☎ 42 8282
🖷 42 8222
@ plavn@molnet.co.mv
🛏 48 🍽 ✎
▭ DC, MC, V

In 2001, government-owned, three-star hotel **Kaca Baltka** underwent extensive renovations, including the addition of extra rooms, each furnished with locally-made furniture and decorated with **handicrafts** from some of Jzerbo's leading artists. It is now rated one-and-a-half stars.

✉ 64 Sv Rojal
☎ 41 4895
🖷 41 4896
@ kaca@moldi.co.mv
🛏 40 ✎
▭ MC, V

$ Accommodation **Budget**

Almost in the centre of town, just a short walk from the railway station, you'll find **Pensjon Klajmazcis**, a rather grim-looking but clean private hotel. Despite its somewhat noisy location, the rooms here are all sound-proofed, which makes them very popular with **honey-mooners** and members of the Jzerbo underworld.

✉ *89 Bvd Busjbusj*
☎ *49 2206*
🖷 *49 2207*
@ *klam@molnet.co.mv*
🔑 *26* 🍴
▤ *DC, MC, V*

Another good-value option for those prepared to stay a little out of town is **Tija**, a modest three-storey hotel to Jzerbo's south. The place may lack a few touches of luxury (i.e. bring your own linen) but this is more than compensated for by the friendly, well-trained staff who will help with sightseeing and can arrange for guests to rent everything from mountain bikes to young boys.

✉ *186 Sv Agtul*
☎ *42 2406*
@ *tija@molnet.co.mv*
🔑 *86* 🖉
▤ *V*

Located just across the river from the Old Town, **Hostjl Latjavko** is a dormitory-style facility that attracts large numbers of backpackers and wasps. There are 50 bunk beds available here, meaning the hostel is officially licensed to accommodate 2000 guests.

✉ *86 Sv Rojal*
☎ *41 9206*
🖷 *41 9207*
🔑 *50*
▤ *MC, V*

As mentioned above, accommodation options outside Jzerbo are pretty limited, but one place worth a mention is **Rjusta Jzarmac**, a newly-opened *aggro-turizm* centre some 60km west of the city. It's basically a working farm full of rustic features where guests get to stay in rooms above the barn, eat meals with the family and help them slaughter livestock.

✉ *25 Sv Hetski*
☎ *44 2158*
⛺ *6*

Note: The place is open year-round, but if you're thinking of dropping in it's a good idea to call in advance so they can reserve a bed and chain up the dogs.

Farmstay accommodation is widely available throughout the Great Central Valley. However, standards may vary from region to region.

WHERE TO EAT

As with its hotels, Jzerbo has struggled to keep pace with the tourism boom when it comes to fine dining. But visitors prepared to be a little adventurous and explore the city's **gastronomical offerings** will not be disappointed. Several high-quality restaurants have recently opened or been re-opened following a **Department of Sanitation** all-clear. There are also numerous *tavernjas* about town offering authentic regional fare, often accompanied by live folk dancing. Remember, if a local artist performs at your table, good manners dictate that you give a tip; the amount depends on whether the performance takes place next to your table or on top of it.

As far as drinking goes, don't forget that Jzerbo wines are fairly robust, with an **alcohol content** of around 15–18%. Beers are a little lighter (5–6%), and then of course there's always the local mineral water (3.5%).

$$$ Dining **Luxury**

Despite the location of **Bouljvard N10**, right on Jzerbo's main square, noise from the passing crowds can barely be heard inside this elegant eatery. Unfortunately, the same cannot be said of the noise from resident pianist, Iobor Jzerbcej, whose love of Molvanian marching music makes for somewhat strident listening.

✉ *10 Bvd Busjbusj*
☎ *48 3145*
▤ *MC, V*

This is another of Molvania's popular 'elevated' eateries. **Bistroj Skie-Hi** is perched a stunning 85m in the air, atop the swaying frame of Jzerbo's telecommunications tower. This exclusive restaurant is one of the city's most popular and expensive. Certainly not a place for those suffering from vertigo, the views from any of the window seats are stunning. Bookings are essential and the dress code stipulates all diners must wear a safety harness.

✉ *78 Av Vrutken*
☎ *43 7375*

Ponj Vredjom, as its name suggests, is built on a bridge overlooking Jzerbo's River Vredom. Water views are a feature at this stylish cafe, whether it's the front window seats offering sweeping vistas of city lights reflected in the river, or the back tables overlooking an outlet pipe from the men's urinals.
Note: The 'Ponj' also has an excellent wine list, provided you intend drinking spirits.

✉ *4 Ponj Vredjom*
☎ *41 3345*

$$ | Dining **Mid-Range**

Pjojo Buz is a ground-level restaurant serving typical Jzerbo dishes – large, high in cholesterol and luke-warm – and is popular with local showbiz personalities, many of whom can be seen serving behind the bar. Despite its casual feel, there is a fairly strict dress code here, requiring men to wear a jacket and shoes.

✉ *57 Sv F.Castro*
☎ *48 3145*

Friendly, family-run bistro **Gosttilja pri Plavjo** is generally full year-round, due no doubt to its excellent food and the fact it only has two tables. The chef's specialty for two, *szijka*, consists of mixed sausages, steak and shish kebabs served with a garnish of rosemary on a sizzling hot-plate. There is a **vegetarian** version but, as it only includes the garnish, non-meat eaters might want to consider an alternative dish.

✉ *35 Bvd Busjbusj*
☎ *45 9595*

$ | Dining **Budget**

Arja Tavernja is a traditional pub-style establishment. A string of cowbells clangs as you open the heavy wooden door and a waitress will pour you a glass of homemade red wine. On no account should this be drunk. The walls are covered with the furs of local wildlife and these **uncured hides** exude an air of rustic authenticity along with a distinct aroma of rotting flesh. Whilst pungent, at least it distracts from the aromas emanating from the restaurant's kitchen. But the food is at least hearty and we can safely say you won't find better stewed goose giblets anywhere in Europe.

✉ *70 Av Vrutken*
☎ *45 3846*

Don't be fooled by the sign outside seedy **Bistroj Bzorzo's** advertising 'topless staff'. Many of them are quite elderly and all are men whose commitment to the hospitality industry would seem fleeting at best. This aside, the food is okay and you should look out for the '**Special of the Day**' display board which, according to several reports, was last updated in 1976.

✉ *145 Sv G.Estefan*
☎ *44 2615*

HIGHLIGHTS

Like most large Molvanian towns, the centre of Jzerbo is dominated by an impressive **cathedral**, dedicated to the city's protector, Saint Cvorbcek. The cathedral is open to the public each morning from 8am and it's worth getting there early as the place can get rather crowded with tourists. (Remember – no singlets, sandals or nipple-rings.) At the front of the church's entrance you will often see a **toothless beggar** hissing profanities at passers-by. He is the local bishop.

Inside the magnificent Baroque cathedral you'll immediately be struck by the massive **organ**, which was designed and built in 1884 by the Molvanian instrument-maker **Jurjst Yvenc** of Lutenblag. With four manuals and pedal board, 6718 pipes (ranging in size from 10m to 13m) and 124 stops, it is one of the largest organs in Europe yet, strangely, is capable of producing only a thin, reedy squeak.

The nearby **Chapel of St Anjevlik** was built between 1622 and 1636, while work on its sumptuous interior continued for another decade. The stunning ceiling frescoes were painted by the Italian master Iacinto Campana and include *The Baptism of Christ* and *The Death of St Peter*. Art historians are, however, divided over whether the same artist contributed to a portrait in the vestry titled *Nude Girl Riding Horse on Beach*.

Museum director Krisjanis Burzjen.
(Photo courtesy 'Molvania's Most Wanted'.)

Culture lovers should consider a visit to Jzerbo's **Krisjanis Burzjen Memorial Museum**. This little-known exhibit is located in the flat (No. 5) occupied by Krisjanis Burzjen himself, Molvania's most famous collector of oral literature. The museum recreates his life and work, and is well worth a visit, although female visitors are warned that if Mr Burzjen invites you upstairs to view his 'folkloric display' it is best to go in a group.

Also close to the centre of town is the Jzerbo **Museum of Natural History**. This museum has permanent exhibitions of geology, entomology and anthropology, as well as an extensive **herbarium** display. You certainly won't be bothered by crowds here as the museum has never had a visitor.

One of the most beautifully preserved thoroughfares in Jzerbo is the **boulevard** running along the southern side of the **Vredjom Park**. In addition to the cafes and antique shops, there are also several attractively restored historic houses in this street, including a large bluestone villa that was once occupied by the city executioner until the position was abolished in 1993.

True Faith...

St Cvorbcek is the locally born saint and protector of Jzerbo, and images of this heavily bearded figure can be seen throughout the city. She was born in 1398, a simple peasant girl, but soon developed a reputation as a devout mystic who would regularly fall into a deep trance and have visions, many of them involving naked men. Devotion to St Cvorbcek reached a peak early last century when a statue of her outside Jzerbo apparently began to weep. Thousands of believers braved the hazardous journey and high ticket prices to make a pilgrimage to this holy shrine, and numerous miracles were attributed to the saintly image. Crowd numbers dropped off in the 1980s when scientific investigations revealed that the statue's tears were triggered by a coin-operated pump but, even today, worshippers still visit this blessed monument.

Not one for the faint-hearted, Jzerbo is home to one of the largest and most popular **stajbulek** (bull-fighting) stadiums in all of Europe. Molvanian bull-fighting differs from the Spanish version in a number of ways: for a start, the *matjeodor* (or bull-fighter) rides a three-wheeled trail bike and, instead of teasing the bull with a red cloak, he controls it with a long-handled **electric cattle prod**. Naturally, the crowd loves every minute of this unique spectacle and will often wage large sums of money on how many minutes the animal will last before going into cardiac arrest.

On the western outskirts of the city is a large park featuring ponds, fountains, picnic facilities and a **forest cemetery**. Many famous Jzerbo residents have been buried in this pine forest, including writer Vorj Dragkot, chess champion Illjia Ggrezel and the great stage actor Hernj Hkorml, who later had to be dug up after **forensic tests** revealed he was not dead but simply in the middle of a dramatic pause.

Surrounding much of Jzerbo is a deep moat filled with stagnant water that gives off a putrid smell. Be careful to keep well clear – not only is it dangerous, this is the town's main water supply.

GYRORIK

Gyrorik is often called the 'Gateway to Molvania' and, certainly, if you were wandering aimlessly south across the barren plains of the **Torzjeccim swamplands** this could well be considered an accurate description. Apart from being one of Molvania's oldest cities, it also the country's most multicultural, with people from Poland, Slovakia, Hungary, Estonia and Ukraine all serving time here at the **Gyrorik Criminal Detention Centre** (open for tours Mon–Fri, please do not feed the inmates).

With wide, tree-lined boulevards, numerous gardens and parks, and a **riverfront boardwalk**, Gyrorik would easily be one of the most visually charming cities in Molvania. Sadly, most of these features were either destroyed or obscured during the 1970s **development boom**, and without them it's a pretty grim industrial centre. Of course, those who do come to Gyrorik and are prepared to look between the pockets of heavy industry and bleak high-rise housing will discover a very special city full of fascinating attractions. There is the **Gyrorik War Museum**, which features a massive exhibition devoted entirely to the **Molvanian Riflemen's Regiment** who fought so valiantly for their country during World War II until their desertion en masse to the Nazis in 1943. On **Memorial Day** you'll see as many people laying flowers on the monument as throwing fruit at it. Festivals are also a big part of city life in Gyrorik and often the streets will be filled with a long and **colourful parade** of people shouting and honking car horns. This is known as *veerjkul* (peak hour).

Gyrorik is surrounded by the picturesque Nonjdezcrip Plains. Once shunned by tourists, this area has become a popular picnic destination, especially now that radiation levels have dropped to almost below W.H.O. recommended limits.

HISTORY

The village of Gyrorik dates way back to the 3rd century when it was used by goat herders as a place to shelter during the harsh winter months. Archaeologists have found numerous **artefacts** from this period, one of the most famous being a clay figurine of a young shepherd boy that, when filled with water, appears to **urinate freely**. Scholars have identified this as perhaps the world's oldest ceramic novelty toy.

By the 8th century, Gyrorik had developed into a bustling **commercial centre** with its own government, army, diseases and even language. The people were fiercely protective of their city and wary about any outside influences, so much so that in AD 900 Gyrorik announced it was declaring independence from the rest of Molvania. The people and their leaders expected a fierce battle but were surprised when the rest of the country agreed without reservation, even offering to contribute funds to help expedite the process. Shortly afterwards, the **Independent Republic of Gyrorik** came into existence but lasted just three years, after which time residents voted to be re-incorporated back into Molvania.

Despite its isolation, the city of Gyrorik has often led the way in Molvanian history. The country's first official outbreak of **bubonic plague** occurred here. In 1743 street lighting was introduced. In 1744 the entire town burnt to the ground, prompting a re-think on the use of **gun-powder-fuelled lamps**. In the 20th century Gyrorik continued to pioneer modern concepts, becoming the first city in Europe to permit driving on either side of the road and giving **livestock** the vote.

Bustling, busy and bursting with life, Gyrorik is a city just waiting to be explored!

The Mayor of Gyrorik, Mr K.V. Stronzlhem, with his younger son 'Little Leon', cabaret singer and fertilizer salesman.

HOW TO GET THERE

Train The completion of a railway link between Lutenblag and Jzerbo was considered by locals as a great leap forward until it was realized that the line would actually bypass Gyrorik. Passengers may, however, alight at **Trbeki Junction** and complete the remainder of their journey by horse-drawn donkey. Most visitors view this as a charming option, until they realise that it's the only option.

Plane Gyrorik's regional airline GyroProp offers a **daily service** to and from Lutenblag, although passengers have often complained about missing baggage. This problem is no doubt exacerbated by the airline's somewhat unusual habit of carrying their cargo strapped to the roof of the plane. Where possible, take as much as you can on as hand luggage.

A reminder for visitors arriving at Gyrorik Airport – **smoking is prohibited** within the terminal building. However, there is a designated smoking area outside the arrivals hall next to the aviation re-fuelling facility.

Car Despite being a long way from any other urban centre, most of the roads into Gyrorik are well-marked and frequently checked for mines. Of course, drivers should make sure their vehicles are in good condition because even though the **Gyrorik Automobile Club** (GAC) offers emergency roadside assistance, their vehicles are often out of service due to mechanical problems.

HOW TO GET AROUND

The city of Gyrorik boasts one of the most efficient and speedy **underground train networks** in all of Europe. Unfortunately, the service only runs for 2km and is therefore of limited use. Buses are a better option and cabs are plentiful although quite expensive by Molvanian standards (many drivers charge for 'extras' such as seat-belts and avoiding pot-holes).

Cafe Society – Molvania Style!
Caffeine lovers in Gyrorik can order a steaming mug of *kappacinjo*, a locally-brewed coffee topped with a layer of frothy milk uniquely derived from animals infected with mad cow disease.

WHERE TO STAY

There is a wide range of **accommodation options** for visitors to Gyrorik, depending on your budget and personal requirements. Establishments at the higher end of the price range are comparable to luxury hotels in Western Europe, while those at the lower end will give you a taste of what it would have been like sheltering in an underground **Taliban stronghold** during the 2002 invasion of Afghanistan.

Hotels remain the most common form of lodging; however, villa accommodation is becoming **increasingly popular** and it is possible for visitors to Gyrorik to rent a small two-bedroom cottage on the outskirts of town for as little as $200 a week. Of course, be prepared to pay a little more if you want the occupants to move out during your stay.

> **Traveller's Tip...**
> *Visitors to Gyrorik find that it's a good idea to pack a universal drain plug, as plugs are often missing in hotel bathrooms. For that matter, a flashlight, small tool-kit and rope ladder could also come in handy.*

$$$ Accommodation **Luxury**

Close to the centre of town, **Hotjl Prozta** has long been popular with business-people and adulterers. The rooms are spacious and all have high ceilings and even higher mini-bar prices. Contemporary Molvanian artwork can be found hanging in the lobby – as can several guests who were once caught stealing one of the hotel's bathrobes.

✉ 54 Av Nazjonal
☎ 22 7575
🖷 22 7577
@ prozta@mol.co.mv
🔑 46 🍽
🖬 DC, V

With a keen eye to period detail, this disused building has been painstakingly restored to its original form. Why the owners of **Spakiegjo** bothered is a mystery as the place was only built 12 years ago and used to be a video rental shop.

✉ 23 Sv Bruce Lee
☎ 24 5804
🖷 24 5805
@ spak@molnet.co.mv
🔑 16 🍽 🖉 🖬 DC, V

The **Gyrorik Holidaj Injn** is exactly what you'd expect from this respected hotel chain, although there are a few interesting local touches – stalactites, for example. Service can be a little slow, and if you plan on using the hotel's only elevator it's worth booking a day or two in advance.

Note: Health facilities include a basement swimming pool and three bars.

✉ 78 Av Busjbusj
☎ 28 0539
🖷 28 0555
@ inn@moldi.co.mv
🔑 94 🖉
🖬 MC, V

$$ Accommodation **Mid-Range**

Gbocjan Mic is a recently built hotel, opposite the main square, offering good, value-for-money accommodation close to all the city's attractions. The hotel also features a restaurant, although one reader notified us that the advertised '**folkloric floor-show**' merely consisted of an elderly – and, on most evenings, inebriated – local resident whose rendition of 'traditional ballads' involved little more than shouting *erz vbe irg gugubcelc!* ('show me your brassiere!') at bemused female patrons before collapsing at the bar.

✉ *12 Sv Mao Tse Tung*
☎ *25 0951*
@ *mic@molnet.co.mv*
🖉 *24*
🖃 *V*

Aranjy Palatz is another centrally-located establishment with good sized rooms, many featuring baths and air-conditioning. There is no restaurant or health club; however, guests are entitled to use facilities at Aranjy's affiliated hotel, conveniently located in Budapest.

✉ *60 Av Nazjonal*
☎ *22 0412*
🖷 *22 0411*
@ *aranjy@mol.co.mv*
🖉 *20* 🖃 *DC, MC, V*

A little further out of town on the main road to Lutenblag you'll find **Kaca Sobieje**, a six-storey hotel featuring its own restaurant and sporting facilities. Being so close to the motorway, traffic noise can be a problem in front-facing rooms, so it's worth asking for one at the back where noise from the adjacent steelworks generally drowns out the sound of cars.

✉ *186 Sv Lutenblag*
☎ *22 7575*
🖷 *22 7577*
@ *sobie@molnet.com*
🖉 *129* 🖉
🖃 *MC, V*

Although it retains traces of its earlier grandeur, the **Jborkle Palatz** is now struggling to maintain standards. An extensive renovation during the 1970s managed to preserve many original features, such as the impressive **marble staircase**, but somehow managed to remove others, such as several **retaining walls**. As a consequence the building now has uneven floors and a leaking roof, although it's not all bad – several of the cracks in the front wall afford excellent views out over a nearby park.

✉ *90 Sv Czokrak*
☎ *28 1563*
@ *jbork@moldi.co.mv*
🖉 *43*
🖃 *V*

> **Philippe writes...**
> ❝ *I first visited Gyrorik in 1976 when there was not a single hotel. So there.* ❞ P.M.

$ Accommodation **Budget**

A Molotov cocktail's throw from the centre of town, you'll find the **Miltajkadetka**, a former defence facility that has been turned into a government-run youth hostel. The rooms are all small but very quiet, not surprising given that most of them are **concrete bunkers** deep underground. Several original features of the facility remain open to guests such as the mess hall (now a cafe) and **obstacle course** (now the lobby).

✉ *37 Sv Bruce Lee*
☎ *20 7423*
✆ *20 7422*
@ *gruc@mol.co.mv*
🛏 *142*

Note: Sadly, the very popular rifle range has recently been closed down following complaints from the primary school next door.

The other main hostel in Gyrorik, the privately-run **Bejcelzet**, is a little further out of town but probably offers better facilities. It has its own games room and Internet cafe, as well as a budget body-piercing clinic.

✉ *104 Ul Pizpiz*
☎ *27 9870*
@ *bejc@net.co.mv*
🛏 *86*
💳 *DC, MC, V*

Note: The proprietor, a former Assistant Commissioner of Police, is a good source of information about the area, especially if you're after drugs.

Those interested in a taste of rural living will find it at **Boricja Manor**, a tourist farm complex some 75km south of the city. Here you can stay in converted stables and experience life on the land as you watch the farmer lovingly tend to his 10,000 battery hens. Of course, like many rural businesses, Boricja Manor does not accept credit cards. Payment here is strictly in cash or cigarettes.

✉ *34 Sv Onslo*
☎ *23 2325*
🐎 *6 stables*

Al fresco dining – Gyrorik style!

WHERE TO EAT

Like many cities in Molvania, Gyrorik's dining scene is developing rapidly as restaurateurs respond to changing tastes and advances in food hygiene. But old habits die hard, and Gyrorik is not the place to eat if you're into low-fat fare. Fried, fatty foods, red meat and **rich desserts** still dominate most menus, although, in a move towards healthy living, many restaurants are now installing cardiac defibrillator machines in their kitchens. Of course, what better way to complement your meal than with a glass or three of Gyrorik wine? Bottles of this **heavily-fortified alcohol** can be found at most licensed grocers or in the paint-stripper section of any hardware shop. And to finish off that special night out? Try a soothing cup of *tzerca*, a locally-grown herbal tea with distinct medicinal qualities – it induces vomiting.

$$$ Dining **Luxury**

Many come to **Starejo Miaska** purely for the atmospheric setting: candlelit bare-brick cellars in one of the most historic manors in downtown Gyrorik. But the food is also excellent, with fresh poultry a specialty. Not only can you choose your chicken or pheasant from a cage, the chef will also let you kill it yourself, considered a great honour. A **string trio** would add a sophisticated touch – if it weren't for the fact they're all banjo players.

✉ 24 Sv Dipterja
☎ 29 8872
🗐 DC, MC, V

Oceajana is in the centre of town. Despite its location some 2000km from the nearest ocean, this ambitious street-front bistro offers an extensive range of succulent seafood. According to several reports, their sushi platter is to die for. Literally.

✉ 23 Av Nazjonal
☎ 21 9961
🗐 MC, V

A short walk from the Gyrorik Museum, you'll find one of the city's culinary institutions, **Qchinzja**. Primarily a steak house, meat features heavily in most dishes here, including dessert.

✉ 17 Av Nazjonal
☎ 23 6986
🗐 MC, V

Note: Those on a kosher diet be warned – the platter of 'traditional grilled meats' may contain traces of cured pig's penis.

TRAVEL ALERT!
A COMMON WAY FOR RESTAURANTS IN MOLVANIA TO ATTRACT TOURISTS IS BY PROVIDING DANCERS IN 'TRADITIONAL COSTUME'. SADLY, IN PARTS OF GYRORIK, THAT COSTUME SEEMS MORE AND MORE OFTEN TO INVOLVE A BRA AND CROTCHLESS PANTIES WHICH, NO MATTER HOW LIBERAL YOUR INTERPRETATION OF MOLVANIAN HISTORY, IS NOT STRICTLY AUTHENTIC. IT IS ALSO DEMEANING ATTIRE FOR THE MEN FORCED TO WEAR IT.

$$ | Dining **Mid-Range**

Bzorgas is a casual eatery just a few doors up from the Town Hall, popular with locals and visitors alike. Freshness is a feature here, with all meals de-frosted on the spot. In summer this relaxed bistro spills over onto the cobbled square outside where patrons will often break into song or hand-to-hand combat, depending on how much they've drunk.

✉ *78 Sv Frokstok*
☎ *29 5961*

Kazminc Jboba is in the centre of the busy district just north of the river. You'll find this unpretentious *tavernja* packed with locals enjoying **Gyrorik specialties** such as *hzermul* (brains fried in garlic), *ezikj* (tongue), *scklat jcumba* (spicy entrails soup) and *prochza* (cheese with gizzards).

✉ *56 Sv Frokstok*
☎ *22 1853*

Note: For the less adventurous diner there are more conventional offerings such as steak and chicken, but even these are generally served on a bed of zmecj (sheep mucus).

Just off Ul Vzitmena in the heart of Old Gyrorik you'll find the stylish **Branjkso** dining hall. With more than 50 main course meals to choose from, this is not the place to go if you have trouble making up your mind. Fortunately, 48 of the dishes involve pickled herring, so it makes the decision a little easier.

✉ *78 Sv Frokstok*
☎ *29 5961*

$ | Dining **Budget**

Yankjees is a newly-opened diner offering what it calls 'Molvanian–American cuisine', a culinary hybrid involving such rarities as beetroot pizza, mule-burgers and spring-onion sodas. However, due to the chef's somewhat literal interpretation of foreign recipes, '**hot-dogs**' are best avoided.

✉ *21 Sv Bruce Lee*
☎ *27 6583*

Another low-cost eating option can be found at **Vvaji's**, a funky little cafe offering excellent food and service in a friendly, windowless setting. There are plenty of tables and it's even cheaper if you're prepared to sit at the bar or on the chef's lap. They also have an **attractive terrace** for open-air eating in summer, although the wasps, midges, sandflies and gypsy beggars can somewhat detract from the ambience.

✉ *30 Sv Mao Tse Tung*
☎ *25 2362*

HIGHLIGHTS

Despite its reputation as an industrial city, Gyrorik is also well known for having one of the largest and most beautiful **botanic parklands** in central Molvania. The 44 hectare **Hopzebja Gardens** attracts people of all ages, who come here to walk, picnic, play frisbee and dump stolen motor vehicles in a shaded, graceful setting.

Branching Out!

The Hopzebja Gardens contain a wide range of trees native to Molvania, including several species that are found nowhere else in the world, such as the Brittle-Boughed Elm, the Splintered Pine and the Bouncing Willow. But the most famous specimen would have to be a 150-year-old Rootless Oak, said to be the slowest growing hardwood in the world. During the 18th century, timber from this tree was highly sought-after by Molvanian ship-builders who would use its short, stunted branches to burn in their stoves.

Of course, Gyrorik was the birthplace of Molvania's most famous composer, **Tzozar Czevkel** (1772–1821), and one of the most beloved sights in the park is the **Czevkel Memorial**, a magnificent bronze statue showing the musical genius in a typical pose – with his pants around his ankles, a bottle of brandy in one hand and a young gypsy boy in the other.

Gyrorik's Old City is home to many architectural highlights, including the **municipal clock** that was built by local craftsmen in 1421 and is famous for never once having displayed the correct time.

Directly opposite the cathedral is the 16th century **Old Arsenal**, a hybrid Gothic–Renaissance building that is nowadays the home of the **Gyrorik Museum**. The highpoint of this museum is its display of royal artefacts, a collection of gold, silver and embroidery, dating mainly from the 16th century, which was hidden in the walls of the arsenal in September 1939 to protect it from **Russian invaders**. The collection was only discovered again in 1992, ironically by **Russian tradesmen** installing an air-conditioning unit, who immediately made off with most of the treasures. The few items that were left behind now form the basis of the somewhat limited display.

To the east of the Old City is a sprawling **stone compound** made up of forbidding, windowless houses, each surrounded by a high wall covered in scenes depicting **fiery death**, the crucifixion and hell. It was here during the Middle Ages that people suffering from leprosy were banished. Today it serves as a child-care centre.

The **Gyrorik Cathedral** is an imposing and beautiful building set back from the main square. After touring at ground level you can climb the wooden staircase that leads from the sacristy to the cathedral tower where visitors may view the famous **Zjekvel bell**. Kissing the bell is said to bring good luck, although the high rates of herpes simplex infection amongst believers would cast some doubt over this claim.

No visit to Gyrorik would be complete without a trip to its famous **abattoir**, one of the largest and most highly mechanized facilities in Europe. Tours are available (children half price), but it's worth booking early, especially in summer, as this is one of the city's most popular attractions.

Gyrorik's famous nuclear reactor is one of the oldest in Europe, with some cracks dating back to the 1960s.

Chess Master

Gyrorik is, of course, the birthplace of Molvania's most famous chess player, the enigmatic Illjia Ggrezel. A man of almost contradictory achievements, he became an international Grandmaster at 12 yet failed his driving licence when he was 25. He spectacularly defeated both Victor Kramnik and Gary Kasparov

on his way to the final of the Eastern Bloc Championship in 1998 but tragically forfeited the final after sleeping through his alarm. Ggrezel is perhaps best known for his blazing victories in the 'Man v. Machine' series held in Lutenblag in 2001 in which he took on the Molvanian-built supercomputer, 'Deep Brown'. This computer could make 14 billion calculations before every move but, as this process took several weeks to complete, the machine lost on time default.

A POEM OF FAREWELL

In 1920 Molvania's then poet laureate K. J. Bcekjecmec (right) penned this ode, traditionally recited to visitors leaving or (being deported from) the country.

Farewell oh visitor to our fine land
Soil as much enriched by your standing on it
As you enriched by having it 'neath your
Travelling shoe.

Though we part as friends most true,
Next time we meet may be in battle
And we shall shed each other's blood
And slit each other's throat.

Indeed, our sons will hate each other
As is the way of God and Nature
Just as the Sun despises the Moon
And the Donkey his Ears.

But let us drink now a toast
And wish each other well
Though I place a curse on you and your family,
For all eternity.

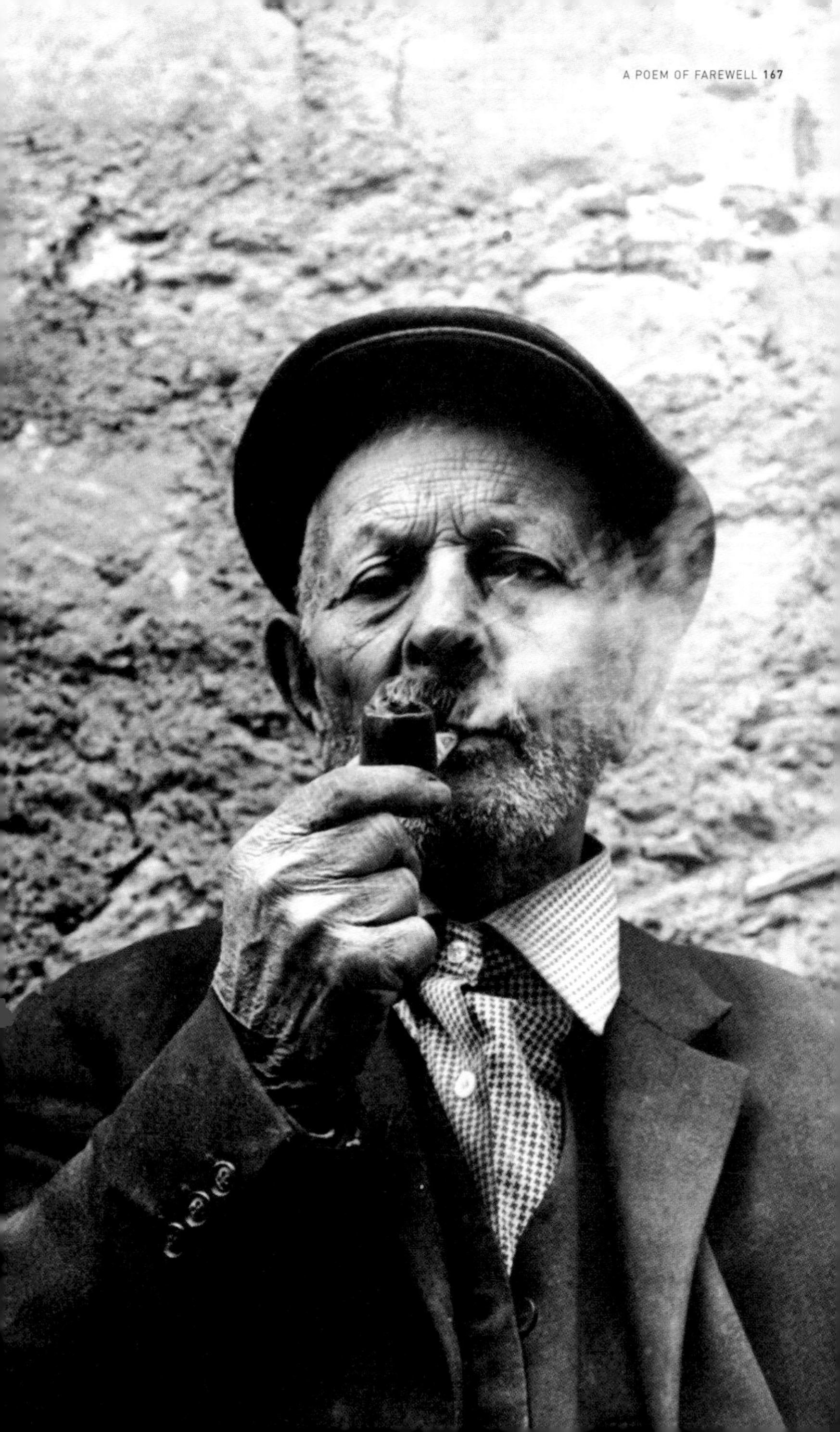

Page numbers in **bold** indicate main references. Page numbers in *italics* refer to maps. Page numbers in ***textile*** are just showing off.

> **Note:** Not all pages correspond to the sections indicated. This is not an editor's mistake, but due to the fact that this book has been printed in Molvania by a company that is very superstitious in matters of numerology.

MAP LEGEND & TEXT SYMBOLS

BOUNDARIES, CITIES & TOWNS

	INTERNATIONAL BOUNDARY
	PROVINCIAL BOUNDARY
	GANGLAND TURF BOUNDARY
✪	NATIONAL CAPITAL
○	PROVINCIAL CAPITAL
●	CITY
•	GHOST TOWN

TRANSPORTATION

	FREEWAY
	MAJOR ROAD
......	MINOR ROAD
	DONKEY PATH
	ESCAPE ROUTE
+++++	RAILWAY – TERRORIST TARGET
	AIRFIELD

AREA FEATURES

Symbol	Description	Symbol	Description
	NATIONAL PARK	~	RIVER
⊛	RADIOACTIVE LAND		LAKE
◇◇◇	UNEXPLORED DUE TO LANDMINES		BOG
	MOUNTAINS		MARSH
	CHEMICAL WASTE DUMP		SWAMP
	NUCLEAR REACTOR		CESSPOOL
			OPEN SEWER

	MINEFIELD WWI
	MINEFIELD WWII
	MINEFIELD (NO REASON)
	MUST SEE ATTRACTION
	WELL WORTH A STOP
	ONLY IF LOOKING FOR A TOILET

MAP SYMBOLS

Symbol	Description	Symbol	Description
	HEALTH SPA		CHURCH/CATHEDRAL
	TOXIC SPA		DEVIL WORSHIP
	RESORT		QUARRY
	NUDIST CAMP		CEMENT WORKS
	PUBLIC TOILET		ENTERTAINMENT
	BANK/ATM		ZOO

	TAXI STAND
	TRAIN STATION
	BUS DEPOT
	AIRPORT
	MUSEUM/GALLERY
	CASINO

TEXT SYMBOLS

Symbol	Description	Symbol	Description
	POST OFFICE/ADDRESS		RESTAURANT
	TELEPHONE		BABYSITTING
	FAX		OUTDOOR DINING
	EMAIL		KARAOKE
	NUMBER OF BEDS		BARN/SHED
	CREDIT CARD	•	HOTEL/INN

MOLVANÎA

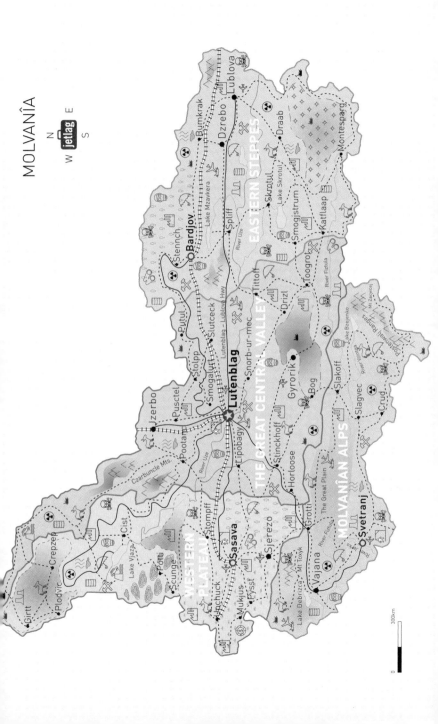

CONVERSIONS

Distance	**Weight**	**Liquid Volume**
Kilometres/Miles/Kraktraks	Kilograms/Pounds/Krakfrigs	Litres/US Gallons/Fizls
$1 = .62 = 1,238^2/_7$	$1 = 2.2 = -139^2/_7$	$1 = .26 = 6$ or 13
		(Depending on whether you're measuring wine or brandy or whether the seller has consumed either)
Metres/Feet/Splutzenfrabs	Grams/Ounces/Plopps	
$1 = 3.3 = 606^2/_7$	$1 = 0.4 = {}^2/_7$	

Women's Clothing

US	UK	EUROPE	MOLVANIA
4	6	34	Not available
6	8	36	Not available
8	10	38	Not available
10	12	40	Small
12	14	42	Medium
14	16	44	Pregnant

Men's Suits

US	UK	EUROPE	MOLVANIA
4	6	34	Not applicable
36	36	46	Not applicable
38	38	48	Not applicable
40	40	50	Not applicable
42	42	52	Not applicable
44	44	54	Not applicable

Temperature

F°	0	10	20	30	32	40	50	60	70	80	90	100
C°	-17.8	-12.2	-6.7	-1.1	0	+4.4	10.0	15.5	21.1	26.6	32.2	37.7
Zk°	$19^{13}/_{17}$	$22^{13}/_{17}$	$26^{13}/_{17}$	$32^{13}/_{17}$	$40^{13}/_{17}$	$51^{13}/_{17}$	$64^{13}/_{17}$	$77^{13}/_{17}$	(Not applicable)			

Shoe Size

Note: The numbers on shoes are not necesarily the sizes but a code indicating the material they're manufactured from.

IE	6	=	Leather
	7	=	Muleskin
	8	=	Wood
	9	=	Asbestos
	10	=	Sandpaper
	11	=	Concrete

LUTENBLAG TRANSPORT SYSTEM

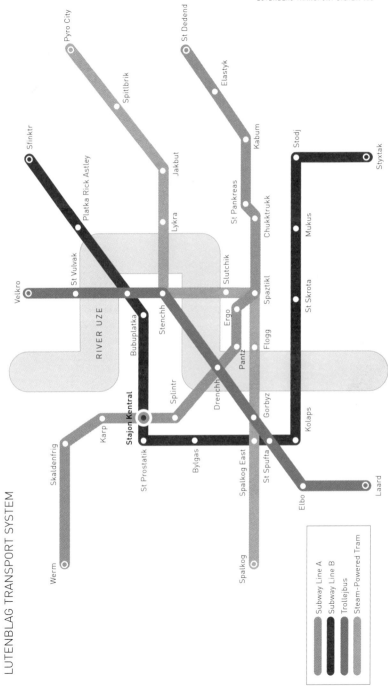

Pyro City
St Dedend
Spitlbrik
Elastyk
Sfinktr
Platka Rick Astley
Jakbut
Kabum
Stodj
Styxtak
St Pankreas
Chukktrukk
Mukus
Lykra
St Vulvak
Velkro
Slutchik
Spaztikl
St Skrota
Ergo
Bubuplatka
Stenchh
Flogg
RIVER UZE
Pantz
Splintr
Drenchh
Gorbyz
Kolaps
Stajon Kentral
Karp
Skaldenfrig
St Prostatik
Bylgas
Spalkog East
St Spufta
Elbo
Laard
Werm
Spalkog

Subway Line A
Subway Line B
Trollejbus
Steam-Powered Tram

Other titles available soon
in the **Jetlag Travel Guide** series...

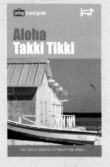

Viva San Sombrero!
CENTRAL AMERICA'S
FORGOTTEN JEWEL...

From the sun-drenched
beaches of Puerto
Polluto to the dazzling
heights of its bustling
capital, Cucaracha City,
this former Spanish
protectorate has well
and truly earned its
reputation as the
region's least war-
ravaged country.

Aloha Takki Tikki!
THE SOUTH PACIFIC'S
FORGOTTEN JEWEL...

Once home to the
fierce Tattoonesian
warriors, this idyllic
French-speaking
island now attracts
sun-lovers and nuclear
scientists alike –
drawn by its warm
waters, iridescent sand
and ever-decreasing
radiation levels.

Let's Go Bongoswana!
Formerly known as
Belgian East Congo,
this mysterious country
has only recently opened
its doors to the world.
From the capital Coup
D'Etat – birthplace
of the safari suit –
to the wild reaches
of the Ebola Jungle,
Bongoswana is just
waiting to be explored.